RACING & RECORD-SE

THE F
TAKERS

A UNIQUE PICTORIAL RECORD 1908–1972

Below From an overall viewpoint, air racing contributed far more to the development of aero-engines than to the aircraft they powered. Perhaps the finest example is that of **Rolls-Royce's Type R** seen here on its Derby test bed in 1929. One of the truely milestone aero-engines of the first half of the 20th century, the Type R was designed to wrest pride of place from the rival Napier Lion engines that had dominated the high powered end of the British air racing scene for most of the 1920s. What Rolls-Royce achieved with the Type R was little short of miraculous. Based on the 825hp Buzzard of 1927, the three-man team of Hives, Lovesey and Routledge started work on the Type R in November 1928, by ignoring the rule book they pushed supercharging pressures to unprecedented heights. By September 1929, the Type R was giving 1,900hp to win that year's Schneider Trophy for Britain, but its development did not end there. Effectively abandoned in the wake of the October 1929 Stock Market collapse, work on the Type R was resurrected in January 1931 and within nine short months the engine was coaxed to give 2,783hp at 3,400rpm and 26lb boost to win the 1931 event, bringing the Schneider Cup permanently to Britain. Of far greater long term importance, however, was the Type R's technological contribution to the war-winning Rolls-Royce Merlin and its own direct development into the Merlin's successor, the Griffon. (Rolls-Royce)

AVIATION PIONEERS 2

RACING & RECORD-SETTING AIRCRAFT

THE RISK TAKERS

A UNIQUE PICTORIAL RECORD 1908–1972

HUGH W. COWIN

First Published in Great Britain in 1999 by Osprey Publishing Limited,
Elms Court, Chapel Way, Botley, Oxford OX2 9LP
Email: osprey@osprey-publishing.co.uk

Text and Captions © Hugh W. Cowin 1999

ISBN 1 85532 904 2

Managing Editor: Shaun Barrington
Editor: Marcus Cowper
Design: The Black Spot
Origination by Grasmere Digital Imaging, Leeds, UK
Printed through Worldprint Ltd, Hong Kong

99 00 01 02 03   10 9 8 7 6 5 4 3 2 1

For a catalogue of all books published by Osprey Military,
Automotive and Aviation please write to:
**The Marketing Manager, Osprey Publishing, PO Box 140,
Wellingborough, Northants, NN8 4ZA, United Kingdom
Email: info@OspreyDirect.co.uk**

**The Marketing Manager, Osprey Direct USA, PO Box 130,
Sterling Heights, MI 48211-0130, USA
Email: info@OspreyDirectUSA.com**

Visit Osprey's website at:
http://www.osprey-publishing.co.uk

The first **Lockheed Sirius**, built to the specifications of its
famed owner, Charles A. Lindbergh. It carried the same NR211
registration that had adorned Lindbergh's Ryan NYP. The Sirius,
with its 450hp Pratt & Whitney Wasp C had a top level speed of
173mph in its early landplane form, as seen here. Accepted by
Lindbergh on 20 April, 1930, he and his wife, Ann Morrow, herself
a pilot, took off for the east coast, setting a new US crossing time
of 14 hours 45 minutes 32 seconds when flying between
Glendale, California and New York, with a single refuelling stop at
Wichita, Kansas. At Ann Morrow's suggestion, NR211 was fitted
with a continuous cockpit canopy in August 1930. In early 1931,
NR211 was put on floats and for the next two years was flown
by the Lindberghs on Pan Am funded surveys of both the Atlantic
and Pacific regions. (Lockheed)

Acknowledgements

My gratitude goes to David Allison, Messrs Andy Bunce, Dave
Charlton and Phil Boydon of British Aerospace, Peter Elliott of
the RAF Museum, J. W. 'Bill' Himmelreich, M. J. 'Mike' Hooks, 'Teddy'
Nevill of TRH Picture and Klaus Peters of Daimler Chrysler
Aerospace for their special support. As ever, I am indebted to
the myriad sources of images that I have been furnished with
over more than forty years and where known, these sources are
quoted in brackets at the end of the caption.

Contents

Hugh W. Cowin was born in January 1934 and spent 12 years in the RAF between 1951 and 1963, mainly with all-weather fighter units. His last five and a half years were spent with the Central Fighter Establishment at RAF West Raynham. He then went into the aerospace industry, culminating in his setting up and heading the Central Market and Research Department for what was to become Lucas Aerospace. A consultant to Fairey Hydraulics since 1972, he retained his pilot's licence and ratings until October 1979. Along the way, he has found time to found *Flight International's* Systems feature, produce the Observer's *Warships* and collect aircraft photographs. Hugh Cowin has also written the first volume in this series, Aviation Pioneers 1: *Research Aircraft 1891-1970: X-Planes.*

Preface

This book is essentially about two of the most glamorous aspects of the history of aviation, air racing and record setting. Although both are now well past their 'glory' years they more than warrant revisiting in order to marvel at the ingenuity and perseverance of the aircraft and engine designers and the sheer courage of the fliers who took these machines aloft.

Air racing emerged earliest, inherently coupled with the initial developments of powered flight. Indeed, the efforts of such pioneers as Henry Farman, Louis Blériot and Glenn Curtiss were directed as much towards winning prizes as developing the field. How many more years, for instance, would the early European designer/aviators, such as Henry Farman have continued to fly straight and unflinchingly ahead, had it not been for the FF50,000 Deutsch-Archdeacon purse awaiting the first to fly a one kilometre closed circuit? Maybe Henry Farman had already acknowledged the need for some form of lateral, or roll control, as argued and even demonstrated by the Wright brothers since 1903, but even if this was so, the lure of the money no doubt spurred things along.

Even in these earliest years, air racing's influence on aviation was to be most felt in the area of aero-engine development, not just in bringing about a need for increased power outputs and improved power-to-weight ratios, but equally importantly, in improving engine reliability.

Turning to air racing's contribution to the airframe, from 1911 onwards, it directed aircraft designers' attention to smoothing the contours and generally attempting to minimise the aerodynamic drag of their machines. Air racing also served to highlight problems – rather than actually solve them – such as wing, tail or control flutter. World War I brought an end to air racing for the duration and when it reappeared it was the government-backed agencies such as McCook Field and later NACA Langley in the US, along with RAE Farnborough and other similar European establishments that were to come up with solutions for such dangerous phenomena, not the air racing fraternity. In fact, by the close of the 1920s, air racing perhaps more than most other sectors of the aviation industry was enjoying the fruits of government agency research, a prime example being the broad-based adoption of the NACA devised long chord radial engine cowling.

As a glance at this book's contents will show, the final section dealing with post-World War II developments is almost totally dedicated to record setting aircraft, with scant mention of air racing. This is not an attempt to disparage latter-day air racing, rather it is a simple acknowledgement that while air racing is alive and well in places like Reno, Nevada, it no longer captures the mass interest it enjoyed in the 1930s, coupled to the fact that as a field of endeavour it has tended to stagnate, most racing being done with modified version of World War II fighters, or lighter-powered machines little removed from the Brown 'Miss Los Angeles' and Chester Jeep-style-setters of the early 1930s. Maybe this was inevitable in the light of the rocketing cost of aircraft development that came about in the wake of jet propulsion. After all, few other than the occasional multi-millionaire such as Darryl Greenamyer could afford to pour the time and money into besting a 30-year-old world speed record for piston engined aircraft, as he did on 16 August 1969 when he flew his much groomed Grumman F8F-2 Bearcat to 483.041mph. It is the huge financial implications of building bigger and better aircraft that have largely precluded progress in air racing since 1945 and why the latter section of this book naturally gravitates towards the kind of machine that only governments could afford to buy and maintain.

Capturing all the fundamental excitement of high powered, low level air racing is this image of a Canadian registered **Supermarine Spitfire FR XIV**, CF-GMZ, rounding a pylon during the qualifying heats for the 1949 Thompson Trophy. Flown by James N. G. McArthur and carrying race no. 80, the machine averaged 370.110mph before being forced to retire. Unlike such American contemporaries as the North American P-51 Mustang and Vought F4U Corsair, remarkably few Spitfires found their way into early post-World War II air racing, making this photograph something of as rarity in itself. (*Cowin Collection*)

Reims and the Aerial Adventurers 1908–1913

The first formal air races were those organised in France during the spring and summer of 1909, although individuals had been flying, again in France, throughout the previous year in attempts to set up some new flying record that usually had some associated prize money. The first reported occasion when several aircraft could be seen flying together was in late May at Port-Aviation near Juvisy; and racing peaked triumphantly in the latter half of August 1909, with the week-long Reims meeting, organised and largely sponsored by the region's champagne industry. In all, some 38 aircraft were entered for the various events, but not all managed to leave the ground. The names of the participating aviators reads like a veritable Who's Who of early heavier-than-air flying and included Blériot, Breguet, Curtiss, Esnault-Pelterie, Farman and Latham. Reims was not only to set the seal of public approval of air racing, it was to foster air racing's expansion outwards by establishing the tradition that the nationality of the winning pilot in a major race would also identify the host nation for the staging of the next event. Thus, despite the name and American nationality of James Gordon Bennett, this Paris-based expatriate first sponsored the Cup that bore his name at Reims in 1909 and it was only as a result of Glenn Curtiss' 1909 winning of the event that it was then held at Belmont Park, New York in the following year.

Just how fast aircraft and their engines evolved over the course of the next five or so years prior to the outbreak of World War I can be gauged by the aircraft types and their performance selected for inclusion within this section.

A particularly evocative image that conjures up the sound and fury of Prevost's winning **Deperdussin** being restrained at the start of the 1913 James Gordon Bennett Cup Race, held that year in Reims, the birthplace of not just French, but air racing everywhere. Note the general modernity of the Deperdussin's lines. (US National Archives)

1

this machine with that of the same machine after extensive modification by Henry Farman in late 1907 and the beginning of 1908 (left). Note the incorporation of outer wing mounted aileron control surfaces that provided the key to Farman's ability to turn with unprecedented ease. (Cowin Collection)

Louis Blériot, born in 1872, had already established his name as a supplier of quality car headlights when he came to aviation in 1905. In that year he became involved with the Voisin brothers,

Left **Henry Farman** holds an anomometer aloft to check wind speed at one of the early French aviation meetings. Like his American contemporary, Glenn Curtiss, Henry Farman and his brother, Maurice, came to aviation via cycling and in Henry's case, fast cars. Initially content to buy his aircraft from the Voisin Brothers, Henry Farman turned to producing his own designs in 1909 after Gabriel Voisin had reneged on the sale of a second 1907 type Voisin to this son of expatriate English parents, by then living in France. Farman started his rise to fame flying his modified 1907 Voisin to record the first one-kilometre (or .62-mile) circuit on 13 January 1908 at Issy-les-Moulineaux, netting him the FF50,000 Deutsch-Archdeacon prize. The flight took one minute 28 seconds, representing a speed of 25.42mph, but far more important than the speed, this achievement indicated that a European had at last managed to break out of the strait-jacket of producing inherently stable aircraft, another way of describing ones that cannot turn or readily recover from a gust-induced side slip. (US National Archives)

Top A line-up of three **1907 Type Voisins**, with that of Henry Farman, carrying the race no. 33, in the middle. Photographed in the late summer of 1907, it is interesting to compare the form of

Charles and Gabriel, and their box kite style gliders. By March 1907, Blériot was learning the hard way by walking away from the crash of his Blériot V canard monoplane. Six months on and his tandem-winged Blériot VI Libellula flew for 604 feet during a number of hops at Issy before crashing. Similar mixed fortunes attended the Blériot VII of November 1907, albeit that its low wing monoplane layout was to influence others. Towards the close of October 1908, Blériot first flew his bi-tailed Type VIII, the machine that nearly killed him in mid-1909, a few weeks prior to his beating Hubert Latham to make the first crossing of the English Channel. (US National Archives)

Louis Blériot was, perhaps, the most prolific of the first wave of French designer/aviators, trying out virtually every type of layout. Here he is seen flying the **Blériot VIII** on his 17-mile cross-country flight of 31 October, 1908. Starting and ending at Toury. This flight marginally exceeded the 16.75-mile flight made by Henry Farman the day before. Nevertheless, it was Farman who took all the glory. (Cowin Collection)

Below and left The two seat **Blériot XII** turned out to be one of the notable aircraft at the August 1909 Reims meeting, beating Glenn Curtiss' machine by just under 1mph to establish the highest speed of 47.8mph. While still at Reims the machine caught fire in-flight and crashed as shown below. Once more, Louis Blériot had a lucky escape with only troublesome burns to the left leg. Maybe it was the publicity surrounding this crash that led to the Blériot XII's limited sales success against that of its immediate forerunner, the Blériot XI, despite its remarkable turn of speed for a two seater. (Cowin Collection)

Above Louis Blériot in his 25hp Anzani powered **Blériot XI**, preparing for his dawn departure on what was to be the first successful crossing of the English Channel, 25 July 1909. Not only did this 36.5 minute flight win him a lasting place in the annals of aviation, it also brought him a purse of £1,000 from the English newspaper the *Daily Mail* and the sort of publicity that would prompt the sale of more than a hundred of these machines, the highest sales of any single type up to that time. With higher powered engines, the Blériot XI would set a number of altitude records over the next two to three years. (US National Archives)

A wet but tenacious **Hubert Latham**, seen here securing his 50hp Antoinette powered Antoinette IV prior to boarding a rescue vessel following his first unsuccessful attempt to cross the English Channel on 19 July 1909, some six days ahead of Blériot's channel crossing. Known as the man who nearly beat Blériot, Hubert Latham, born in 1883, was a relative newcomer to flying, having started in 1908 after having been told he had only a little time to live. Once back in Paris, Latham promptly ordered an Antoinette VII, whose engine once again, uncharacteristically it

should be said, let him down, dunking him and his machine into the Channel when 1.5 miles from Dover on 27 July. Latham, of Anglo-French parents, died in 1912 of injuries inflicted by a buffalo while hunting in America. (Cowin Collection)

Born in 1878, **Glenn H. Curtiss** established his own company in September 1901 and soon progressed from building bicycles to motor cycles and motor cycle racing, using Curtiss engines. On 24 January, 1907, Curtiss, riding one of his own air-cooled engined motor cycles became the fastest human, when he set a new world speed record of 137mph. Already supplying his engines for airship use since 1904, Curtiss was a 'natural' to make the transition into aviation, becoming a founder member of the Aerial Experiment Association on its formation in October 1907. By mid-1908, Curtiss

was aloft in the AEA's 'June Bug', the third and most successful of the AEA designs. Much more of an entrepreneur than the Wright Brothers, Curtiss, when warned by the military at the end of 1912, that his and the Wrights' pusher engined biplane designs were obsolete, took steps to rectify the problem. Whereas the Wrights' company did nothing and essentially vanished from the scene, Curtiss, in 1913, imported a British designer, B. Douglas Thomas, formerly with Sopwith, who drew up the Curtiss Models J and N, from which flowed the Curtiss JN in late 1914. Ultimately to be built in enormous quantities, the JN, more than anything else, established both Curtiss and his company among aviation's great names. (Curtiss)

A little larger than the original Curtiss No.1, the similar **Curtiss-Herring No.1 Reims Racer** was completed in secrecy to represent the US in the first James Gordon Bennett Cup, one of the events in the Reims meeting, held between 22–29 August 1909. Seen here with Glenn H. Curtiss at the controls during the Reims events, Curtiss battled it out, primarily against Louis Blériot, to win the Cup with an average speed of 47.385mph. The Reims Racer was powered by a Curtiss 50hp water-cooled engine and wore the race no. 8. (US National Archives)

Claude Graham-White, seen here in his Henry Farman III, was born in 1879 and grew up with an interest in sports and all things mechanical. Showing an early flair for business, he turned first to ballooning in 1904 and then to heavier-than-air flying, attending the August 1909 Reims meeting, where he bought a Blériot XII two seater, the start of an on-going involvement with flying training. In early 1910, Graham-White bought a Henry

Farman III in pursuit of the £10,000 Daily Mail purse for the first to fly from London to Manchester. Alas, he was to be beaten in the event by Frenchman, Louis Paulhan, but, in the process, was to make the first recorded night take-off, with the aid of car headlights, at 2.45am on 28 April 1910. Graham-White enjoyed greater success in the US later in the year, when he won numerous prizes flying his Blériot XI, including the $10,000 first place award for the 1910 James Gordon Bennett Cup, held on 29 October 1910, at Belmont Park, New York, with an average speed of 61mph. Early in 1911, Graham-White bought the land to set up Hendon Aerodrome. Here he operated his own flying school and aircraft manufacturing business, promoting both air-mindedness and Hendon by holding weekend flying events, including the annual Aerial Derby from 1912. At the outbreak of war, Graham-White joined the Royal Naval Air Service and five months later was among the first British pilots to raid German bases on the Belgian coast. Rescued from a watery forced landing, Graham-White resigned his commission on his return to concentrate on aircraft production, having learnt of plans to put him in command of an armoured train. Never one to suffer fools gladly, Graham-White became embroiled in an extended struggle with the British Government in the wake of the Armistice concerning compensation for aircraft contract cancellations and the return to him of Hendon, requisitioned on 4 August 1914. Ultimately resolved in his favour, this protracted battle saw Graham-White abandon aviation and Britain in 1929 to devote his time to property development. (Cowin Collection)

Orville Wright is seen here at the controls of the **Wright Baby Racer**, present at the 1910 James Gordon Bennett Cup race, but not entered to race, perhaps in deference to their father's attitude to any form of gambling (he was a Baptist Minister). As it was, the Baby Racer gave a good account of itself during demonstration flights, being unofficially timed at 70mph, some 9mph faster than Claude Graham-White's Cup winning speed. Note the fact that the machine was still a pusher-engined biplane, with wing warping and, other than in using wheels, ignored the tractor-engined monoplane layout advances being made in Europe. (US National Archives)

Overleaf Born in 1886, **Eugene Ely**, seated at the controls with Glenn Curtiss standing alongside, had joined the Curtiss Exhibition Company soon after its formation in July 1910 Ely's name came to prominence as the first aviator to take-off and land an aircraft aboard ship, respectively, from the cruiser USS Birmingham on 10 November 1910 and onto the USS Pennsylvania on 18 January 1911. Prior to these events, Ely had

broken the conservatism of US aircraft design by having Curtiss convert one of his standard pusher biplanes into a pusher monoplane. Sadly, Ely was to be killed during an exhibition flight at Macon, Georgia on 19 October 1911. (US National Archives)

Bottom The rather bizarre looking **Ely Monoplane**, photographed at Belmont Park on 28 October 1910, the day before that year's James Gordon Bennett Cup and for which it had been entered. As it transpired, the Ely Monoplane did not fly in the race. (Curtiss)

Above right This Gnome rotary powered **Morane-Borel**, flown by Jules Vedrines, was the only machine to complete the Paris to Madrid air race. Delayed by a day following the death of the French War Minister, the race went off on 22 May 1911. It took Vedrines four days to complete the journey. (US Air Force)

Below This, the second of **Edouard Nieuport** monoplane designs, his 1910 monoplane set new standards in drag reduction. Flown with progressively more powerful engines,

starting with an 18hp Darracq. However, by the time this photograph of Charles Weymann flying his Nieuport to victory in the 1911 James Gordon Bennett Cup was taken, the machine was wearing a 100hp Gnome rotary. Weymann's winning speed was 78mph. Edouard Nieuport, born in 1875, was to be fatally injured, when he stalled his aircraft during demonstrations to the French military on 16 September 1911.

Above Photographed at Hendon in 1913, this **Morane Saulnier Type H** single seater, piloted by Frenchman Brindejonc des Moulinais, is being anchored by volunteer helpers against the pull of its 80hp Gnome. First flown in 1912, the Type H went on to win many races around Europe, including the 1912 and 1913 Aerial Derbies organised by Claude Graham-White.

Right **Roland Garros**, born in 1888, was one of the many to attend the August 1909 Reims meeting and, forsaking his erstwhile ambitions to become a concert pianist, shortly afterwards bought a Santos-Dumont Demoiselle and learnt to fly at Issy. Clearly destined for great things, Garros set a new world altitude record of 12,828 feet on 4 September 1911, flying a Blériot XI. On 17 September 1912, he broke his earlier record with a height of 17,880 feet, flying a Morane Saulnier. Just over a year on and Garros was to become the first aviator to cross the Mediterranean non-stop, when, on 23 September 1913, he flew the 453 miles between southern France and Tunisia. As a military aviator, Garros helped perfect an armoured propeller cuff, allowing him to aim the whole aircraft when firing at his prey. Between 1–18 April 1915, Garros downed five German two seaters, before being downed himself. Taken prisoner, Garros escaped in early 1918 to return to combat flying. Sadly, this implacable aviator was shot down and killed on 5 October 1918, just over a month prior to the Armistice. (US National Archives)

Above Roland Garros, photographed in June 1913, sitting in the **Morane Saulnier Type H** in which he made the first non-stop crossing of the Mediterranean. Departing Saint Raphael in south eastern France on the morning of 23 September 1913, with 55 gallons of fuel, Garros wisely flew a route that took his 60hp landplane over Corsica and Sardinia. On reaching Bizerta in northern Tunisia, Garros had one gallon of fuel remaining.

Maurice Prevost banks his very clean looking **1913 Deperdussin Monocoque** around one of the course marker pylons on his way to winning the 1913 James Gordon Bennett Cup at Reims. Held on 29 September, Prevost's machine was powered by 160hp two-row, contra-rotating Gnome rotary and his winning speed was 124.5mph over this 124.3 mile course. The superb contouring of this monoplane poses the question: why did many designers soon revert to the biplane layout for their military aircraft? The primary consideration was strength, the biplane offering a very robust, rigid wing structure. (US Air Force)

The 'Roaring Twenties', 1919–1928

In the aftermath of World War I, air racing grew in popularity within the **US**, while never quite regaining the mass appeal it had enjoyed in Europe. The reasons for this disparity are many and complex, but high on the list must be the differing cultural approaches to the sport. The American approach was a straightforward one of first-past-the-post wins. This had much

to commend it, particularly in terms of public spectacle. The European approach was to attempt to impose an arbitrary level of equality throughout the sport, and by the mid-1920s they were dreaming up progressively more stringent rules for handicapping race entrants. This certainly allowed a far greater variety of machines to take part as is shown in this section,

it did, however, frequently tend to penalise the faster types.

Interestingly, American air racing in the period being reviewed here was actually dominated by the armed forces, civilian air racing did not really make its debut before 1929. This military participation, dominated by the Army versus Navy rivalry, enhanced the competition for the viewers, regardless of the individual aircraft's actual performance.

As the story of the Verville Sperry R-3 highlights, the airframe innovations brought about in producing such a thoroughbred racing machine were to have little impact in advancing the more conservative military designs.

Without question, much of the contribution air racing made to aviation development, came, once again, in the form of engine development, largely directed at perfecting the higher powered, air-cooled radial.

The Alfred Verville designed **Verville Sperry R-3**, seen here in its later 1923 form, fitted with a 500hp Curtiss D-12. The R-3 had a set of main wheels that retracted inwards operated by hand crank from the cockpit. In the air, the R-3 proved itself capable of speeds approaching 250mph and is seen by many as the true precursor of the modern fighter. As often happens, this extremely promising design was to provide something of a false dawn, with the US military failing to pursue its potential and adhering to the biplane layout for its fighters for the best part of another decade. (US Air Force Museum)

First flown on 5 July, 1918, only two US Navy **Curtiss 18T Wasps**, Bu Aer A3325 and A3326 were to be built Designed as well-armed two seat fighters, their prospects essentially evaporated with the Armistice that November. Happily, the two triplanes, with their 400hp Curtiss-Kirkham K-12 prototype engines were retained as racers and as such raced in both wheeled and floatplane forms. Bu Aer A3325 is seen here just prior to its destruction while taking part in the St Louis races on 6 October 1923. (US Navy)

Below Carrying race no. 5, the first of the two US Navy **Curtiss 18T Wasps**, Bu Aer A3325, is seen taxiing prior to the start of the 1922 Curtiss Marine Trophy race. Both Wasps were entered for the event and both failed to finish, no. 5, flown by Lt. R. Irvine, US Navy, dropping out in the fifth lap, while its sister ship, race no. 4, flown by US Marine Lt. L. H. 'Sandy' Sanderson, left the race while leading and within sight of the finish, when it ran out of fuel. (Curtiss)

Below The exceptionally clean looking Dayton Wright-built **Rhinehart-Baumann RB-1** was certainly the most interesting of the four American entrants for the 1920 James Gordon Bennett Cup, to be held just outside Paris on 28 September. Literally bristling with new ideas, the RB-1 embodied a pair of retractable main wheels and a variable chamber wing. Anticipating the Boeing Krueger flap system by forty years or so, the wing was so designed that the whole leading edge could be drooped in sympathy with the full length flaps-cum-ailerons to increase lift and allow the machine to land at a lower airspeed. In the event, the RB-1, race no. 2, was forced to drop out of the race when pilot Howard Rhinehart found the 250hp Hall-Scot engined machine to be barely controllable. Apparently airflow disruption over the upper fuselage exacerbated a bad case of under-finning. Just why the RB-1 was allowed to get as far as France before discovering these problems remains unanswered. (US Air Force Museum)

Above The last of four **Bristol M.1Ds**, the ill-fated G-EAVP, being manhandled across Plough Lane, Croydon just prior to the 1923 Grosvenor Cup race, held on 23 June. Essentially a de-militarised Bristol M.1 scout fitted with a 140hp Bristol Lucifer radial, G-EAVP had won the last of the Hendon Aerial Derbies, when, on 7 August 1922, it had romped home with an average speed of 108mph. Flown by Major Leslie Foot in the 1923 Grosvenor Cup, the machine crashed and burned near to the end of the Bristol-Croydon leg, killing its pilot, who had only recently joined Bristol from Handley Page. (Cowin Collection)

The **Sopwith Gnu** three seater, G-EAGP, seen here at Croydon on another occasion, was the unlikely winner of the 1923 Grosvenor Cup event that had been marred by the tragic death of Major Leslie Foot. Powered by a 110hp Le Rhone rotary, the Gnu was credited with a top speed of 93mph. (Cowin Collection)

Above The sole **Bristol Bullet**, G-EATS, owed its existence to Roy Fedden of Bristol's recently formed Aero Engine Department, who needed a fast, agile machine to serve as a flying test bed for his Cosmos, later Bristol Jupiter, radial. Clearly, Fedden argued, producing a racer would provide the harshest of test conditions and any wins would be a publicity bonus for the overall Bristol organisation. First flown in mid-1920, with Cyril Uwins at the controls, the Bullet as originally configured proved a disappointment, only managing third place in the 1920 Aerial Derby, held on 24 July. On this occasion, the Bullet clocked 129mph with Uwins flying it. Having undergone fairly drastic surgery to its wings and tail unit, the Bullet, now with a 450hp Bristol Jupiter II, re-emerged in the guise seen here, taking second place in the 1921 Aerial Derby, at 141mph and this time, stripped of its massive airscrew spinner, came second again in the 1922 Aerial Derby, averaging 145mph. (Bristol)

Overleaf The trim looking **Gloster Mars I**, or Bamel, G-EAXZ, was built to compete in the 1921 Aerial Derby, being powered by a 450hp Napier Lion II. First flown on 20 June 1921, the sole Mars I went on to win that year's Aerial Derby, held on 17 July,

23

with a speed of 163.3mph. On 19 December 1921, the Mars was timed at 196.4mph to set a new national speed record and the Mars, once again, romped home on 17 August, to win the 1922 Aerial Derby, with a speed of 177.8mph. It was the success of this machine that was to pave the way for the later series of Lion powered Gloster Schneider Trophy racers. (Gloster)

Seen here about to fly an early production Bristol Blenheim in 1937, **Cyril Uwins** was born on 2 August 1896 and was destined to become one of Britain's earliest and longest serving test pilots. Trained to fly by the RFC in 1916, Uwins fractured his skull in a crash quite early in his flying career, prior to being posted to the Bristol Company on 20 November, 1917. Here he served as the RFC's resident acceptance and ferry pilot. At this point, Uwins' log book shows a total of 258 hours, 5 minutes. Flight testing and delivering numerous Bristol F2Bs added a further 295 hours, 5 minutes by 26 October 1918, when Flg. Off.

Uwins was officially seconded to become Bristol's test pilot. Tall and taciturn, Uwins was not afraid of speaking out when required and, with a few pointed words, could end the career of a design forthwith, as in the case of the Bristol Type 72 Racer. Uwins last flight as a pilot was made in an Airspeed Oxford on 20 October 1951, closing a flying career that spanned 4,500 flying hours on 170 types, including 54 first flights. Uwins went on to become Bristol's Managing Director from 1947 to 1957 and Deputy Chairman from then to his retirement in 1964. The observation that: 'There are bold pilots and old pilots, but few old, bold pilots' is attributed to Cyril Uwins, who died of old age in 1972. (Bristol)

The full rotundity of the sole **Bristol Type 72 Racer**, G-EBDR, can be gauged from these two views of the machine at Bristol's Filton plant. First flown in early July 1922, the Racer was powered by a totally submerged 480hp Bristol Jupiter and embodied a number of novel features, including a retractable landing gear and wing/body blending. Regrettably, as Cyril Uwins was to discover the first time he lifted the Racer off, its full span ailerons twisted the light wing structure alarmingly and induced constant lateral instability. The airscrew spinner burst explosively during the initial climb-out on the second flight, tearing fabric from the port wing and demolishing the pitot/static tube. The fourth flight was particularly alarming, when a cam system introduced to 'gear' aileron response came adrift and left Uwins with virtually no lateral control. After seven short flights, Uwins felt it time to speak up and the Type 72 Racer was quietly abandoned. (Bristol)

Above A proud US Navy Lt H. J. Brow poses with his **Curtiss CR-2**, Bu Aer A6081, in which he took third place on 14 October, 1922, in that year's Pulitzer Trophy. Held over a 155.35 mile course near Detroit, Brow's speed was 193.2mph. The sole CR-2 had started life the summer of the previous year as one of two CR-1s, powered by a 425hp Curtiss CD-12. At this time both machines had their engines cooled by two barrel-like Lasmblin radiators, A6081 became the CR-2 when fitted with the aerodynamically much cleaner Curtiss wing surface radiators in 1922 as seen here. Both US Navy CRs were subsequently converted to floatplanes for the 1923 Schneider Trophy event. (Curtiss)

In the early 1920s, military and naval procurement staff often found it easier to obtain money to buy racing aircraft than to purchase prototype fighters, perhaps because of the publicity value that attached to air racing. Whatever the reason, the US Army's order for three **Verville Sperry R-3s**, purportedly for the prestigious 1922 Pulitzer Trophy was, in fact, a cover to obtain an advanced pursuit design, as Americans then referred to their fighters. Seen here in its initial form with twin Lamblin radiators underslung from beneath the centre section, the R-3 was powered by a 400hp Wright H-3 and was the first US army aircraft to have fully retractable main wheels. Tests with the early R-3 showed its top speed with wheels down to be 162.8mph, while with wheels up, speed increased to 191.1mph. Flown for the first time on 22 September 1922, all three R-3s, AS22-326, 327 and 328, took part in the 14 October 1922 Pulitzer, but their performance was somewhat disappointing, AS22-326, race no. 49, seen here, took fifth place at 181mph, AS22-328, race no. 48, came in seventh at 178mph, while AS22-327, race no. 50, dropped out on the fifth lap when its engine seized up. Before the 1923 Pulitzer Trophy, held on 6 October at St Louis, Missouri, AS22-328 was modified to take the new 500hp Curtiss D-12 Special. On the day, however, AS22-328 could manage no better than to drop out on the first lap with severe airscrew spinner vibrations. AS22-328, this time wearing race no. 70, was to eventually triumph during the 1924 Pulitzer race, held at Dayton, Ohio. Here, on 4 October, the R-3, flown by Lt. H. H. Mills, stormed home to win with an average speed of 215.7mph over the 124.28 mile course. (US Air Force Museum)

Overleaf Not to be outdone by the US Army's R-3s, the US Navy bought two examples of the retractable wheeled **Bee Line** racing monoplane as entrants for the 1922 Pulitzer. While both Bee Lines were powered by the same 390hp Wright H-3, the machines differed in the type of engine radiator fitted. Thus, the **BR-1**, Bu Aer A6429 had twin Lamblins, while the **BR-2**, seen here, adopted the Curtiss wing surface type. Interestingly, according to US Navy figures, the Curtiss type was heavier by 30lb and while looking smoother incurred an 11.4mph penalty in

Not all records were to be set by glamorous, stripped down racers, as demonstrated by this US Army **T-2** cargo 'plane, AS64233, one of two **Fokker F IVs** bought in 1922. To this machine must go the honour of making the first non-stop coast-to-coast crossing of the US. Piloted by Lts. John A. MacReady and Oakley H. Kelly, AS64233 climbed out from Roosevelt Field, Long Island on 2 May 1923, to land 26 hours, 50 minutes later at Rockwell Field, San Diego, some 2,520 miles from its starting point. Powered by a single 420hp Liberty 12A, the T-2 had a top speed of 95mph. (US Air Force)

top level speed. Both Bee Lines failed to finish the race. Incidentally, the forward view-hindering protuberance right in front of the pilot was a housing for the cooling system's expansion tank. (US Navy)

First flown only shortly before the mid-October 1922 Pulitzer Trophy event, two **Navy-Wright NW-1s** had been ordered, but only Bu Aer A6544 was to fly. Compelled to 'ditch' during the race, A6544, race no. 9 was re-built using parts from the incomplete A6543. Designed under the leadership of Rex Beisel, who was to go on to design the Vought F4U Corsair, the NW-1's primary role was to serve as a high speed flight test vehicle for the newly developed 650hp Wright T-2 engine. The NW-1's top level speed was 196mph. During the early part of 1923, the NW-1 was not just re-built, it was transformed from a land-based seaplane into the NW-2 float-equipped biplane backup for the US Navy's three 1923 Schneider Trophy Curtiss entrants. (US Navy)

Opposite **Alfred J. Williams, Jr**, was born in July 1896 and was gifted with an extremely analytical mind. In joining the US Navy in 1917, Williams relinquished a promising career as a pitcher with the New York Giants. As a naval aviator, Williams was quickly recognised for his talent as a combat tactics instructor. Following the Armistice, Williams' role was expanded to include

that of research test pilot. Prominent among the small elite of service racing pilots and growing impatient of the 'Battleship Admirals' mentality within the US Navy, this 'square peg in a round hole' resigned his commission in 1930 to join Gulf Oil as manager of their Aviation Department, where he stayed until the US entered World War II. Then, in an unveiled gesture of disdain for his former service, Williams took unpaid leave from Gulf Oil for the war's duration to teach air combat tactics to US Army Air Force pilots on a voluntary basis. After leaving Gulf Oil in 1951, Williams spent his latter years on his farm. (US Navy)

Below Photographed on 17 September 1923, US Navy Lt. Alfred J. 'Al' Williams stands besides the **Curtiss R2C-1**, Bu Aer A6692, race no. 9, in which he won the 1923 Pulitzer Trophy, with a speed of 243mph. Another R2C-1, Bu Aer A6691, race no. 10, flown by Lt. H. J. Brow came in second, with a speed of 241.78mph, while third and fourth places went to US Marine and Navy pilots respectively, both flying Navy-Wright F2W-1s. The Curtiss R2C-1s were powered by the newly available 500hp Curtiss D-12 Special. (Curtiss)

Below right First flown on 5 May 1926, by Cyril Uwins, the **Bristol Type 99 Badminton** was originally powered by a 510hp Bristol Jupiter VI and was entered for that year's King's Cup. Sadly, luck was not with its pilot, Capt. Frank Barnard, compelled to drop out on the third lap of this 9 July event due to fuel starvation. At Barnard's suggestion, the sole Badminton, G-EBMK, was modified prior to the 1927 King's Cup, being fitted with a set of completely re-designed wings and re-engined with a 525hp Jupiter, as seen here, was re-designated Type 99A in the process. Tragically, Capt. Barnard was killed when the Badminton crashed during pre-race tests on 28 July 1927, following engine failure soon after take-off. (Bristol)

Perhaps the most prolifically built and operated military aircraft of the 1920s and 1930s, the sleek **Breguet Bre 19** sesquiplane was flown by no less than twelve air forces on three continents over a span of 15 years. First flown in May 1922, this two seat light bomber and reconnaissance type used a number of engines, the 450hp Lorraine 12Eb being most favoured, as seen fitted to this Bre 19B, whose top level speed was 140mph at sea level. The Bre 19 appears to have been particularly well suited to long distance flying, setting no fewer than six straight line records between February 1925

and 29 September 1929. Flown by two French Capts., Costes and Bellonte, this last record was for 4,912 miles. Less than a year later, the same pair of airmen, again using a Bre 19, made the first east to west crossing of the Atlantic between 1 and 2 September 1930. (ECPA)

A youthful **Charles A. 'Slim' Lindbergh**, seen here in the place he most liked to be, the cockpit of an aircraft. Born in 1902, Charles Lindbergh learnt the rudiments of aircraft handling and maintenance in 1922, but the company that had promised to train him to fly sold their last aircraft before he had 'soloed'. Undeterred, Lindbergh bought his own machine, a war-surplus 90hp Curtiss JN-4 and set off barnstorming with fare-paying passengers while furthering his piloting skills. In 1924, Lindbergh quit 'barnstorming' and joined the US Army as a trainee pilot at Brook Field, Texas, from where he graduated

in March 1925, going straight into the Air Corps Reserve. This left him free to join Robertson Aircraft, St Louis, as their Chief Pilot in the summer of 1925, where he found himself responsible for starting up an air mail service between St Louis and Chicago and flying it in war-surplus DH 4s regardless of weather and with no aids other than his wits. Twice in a few short months, Lindbergh was compelled to take to his parachute, later retrieving the mail from the wreckage to deliver it as stipulated. In September 1926, Lindbergh started to contemplate alternatives to his current, somewhat hazardous life style and by early 1927 had negotiated time off and some support from Robertson in an endeavour to enter the running for the $25,000 Raymond Orteig purse for being the first to make the trans-Atlantic crossing between New York and Paris, or vice versa. Because of the prevailing winds, the west to east crossing was clearly favoured. The French World War I ace, Rene Fonck had crashed the big three engined Sikorsky S-35 departing Roosevelt Field in September 1926, while Noel Davis and S. H. Wooster, plus Charles A. Levine were announced contenders. Time was not on Lindbergh's side. Belatedly, in February 1927, Lindbergh found someone in the shape of Claude T. Ryan, who would build a machine to his special needs and Lindbergh moved into Ryan's premises in San Diego to supervise construction. On 26 April 1927, Davis and Wooster were to die in their Keystone Pathfinder, while on 8 May news reached Lindbergh of another French air ace, Charles Nungesser, and Francois Coli's departure from Paris. The period from 10 May to his eastbound departure on that momentous 3,590 mile, 33 hour, 39 minute flight on 20 May best characterises Lindbergh the man. Departing San Diego for his St Louis stop-over to New York, Lindbergh showed commendable nerve in nursing his Ryan NYP over tall mountains with a faltering engine. Yet, regardless of press allusions to his being

'the Flying Fool', here was a man quite prepared to grit his teeth for days for just the right weather. Much mythology was soon to surround Lindbergh, but real history shows him in an even more favourable light. (Library of Congress)

The sole **Ryan NYP**, short for New York-Paris, NX211, 'Spirit of St Louis' seen here over San Diego, was ordered by Charles Lindbergh on 28 February 1927 and thoroughly air tested by him prior to his eastbound departure on 10 May. Designed by Donald Hall, later to make his name at Consolidated, the NYP was essentially a totally new design with the exception of its wings ribs and tail unit, both taken from Ryan's M-2. Not very stable, this meant that Lindbergh necessarily had to stay 'hands on' for the whole of the 3,590 mile trans-oceanic flight. While this flight is well documented, less well understood is the fact that Lindbergh, aware of his competitors, took a mere 21 hours, 21 minutes, with a stop-over in St Louis, to fly from San Diego to New York's Curtiss Field. (Ryan Teledyne)

Overshadowed in terms of fame by the later DH 82 Tiger Moth biplane trainer, the **De Havilland DH 71 Tiger Moth**, of which two were built, was drawn up in early 1927 under a veil of secrecy more in keeping with a military machine than a light civil type. The reason for this secrecy centred on Geoffrey de Havilland's desire to produce a high speed aircraft with which to test the new 130hp Halford designed engine that would lead to the famous Gipsy series. First flown on 24 June 1927, the two DH 71s were registered G-EBQU and G-EBRV, the latter retaining an 85hp ADC Cirrus II for comparative purposes. G-EBQU, seen here after being fitted with the new engine, was forced to withdraw from the 1927 King's Cup due to the severity of the weather, but went on to establish a new light aircraft speed record of 186.4mph on 24 August 1927. Incidentally, the DH 71's pilot for the King's Cup was Hubert Broad, who also undertook most of its test flying. (De Havilland)

Previous page **Arthur C. Goebel** on the right, stands with **Walter Beech**, the then President of Travel Air, producers of Goebel's Travel Air 5000 'Woolaroc'. A Hollywood stunt pilot, 'Art' Goebel was propelled to fame by being the winner of the fatality strewn Dole air race, held on 16 August 1927, with its goal of crossing the Pacific from Oakland, California to Hawaii. Absent from this photograph is 'Woolaroc' navigator, 'Bill' Davis. Ironically, two US Army fliers, Lts. L. Maitland and A. Hegenberger, had made the first non-stop flight over this 2,400 mile route on 28–29 June 1927, in an Army three engined Fokker C-2 transport. In the following month, Ernest Smith and Emory Bronte, tired of the Dole race organisers' bureaucracy, took off in another single engined Travel Air 5000 and flew for 25 hours, 36 minutes before making an undignified but safe crash landing in Hawaii. (Beech)

Above **Travel Air 5000**, NX869, 'Woolaroc', normally a pilot, plus four passenger machine was modified for the August 1927 Dole race between California to Hawaii. Inside, cabin space and seating made way for extra fuel tankage and newly devised radio direction finding aids. Laden with fuel, 'Woolaroc' trundled down the yet to be completed Oakland Airport strip, to arrive 26 hours, 17 minutes, 33 seconds later at Honolulu to win the $25,000 winner's purse. Of the eight starters, only one other machine, the Breese Monoplane of Jensen and Schluter was to make landfall in Hawaii to win the remaining $10,000 in prize money. Two aircraft and five lives were to be lost in the course of this event set up by Hawaiian pineapple magnate, James D. Dole. (Beech)

The sole **Blackburn Lincock I**, seen here prior to having its G-EBVO registration applied, was a company funded lightweight, low powered fighter designed to appeal to smaller nation users. Completed and first flown in the spring of 1928, the Lincock I had a 240hp Armstrong Siddeley Lynx IVc, giving it a maker's quoted top level speed of 146mph. Normally, maker's figures tend to be on the optimistic side, but in this case, it seems that Blackburn were erring in favour of conservatism, as the Lincock was placed 10th in the 1928 King's Cup with an average speed of 145.32mph. (Blackburn)

Right A two seat **Curtiss F8C-1** of the US Marine Corps banks around one of the pylons at the Los Angeles-based 1928 National Air Races. Military entrants such as this were to dominate American air racing through most of the 1920s. All this was to change dramatically in 1929 with the debut of the Travel Air Model R. This machine was to change the face of American air racing virtually single-handedly and ushered in an era of high powered, high speed civilian racers that relegated the military to a supporting air display role.

DELCO LIGHT

The Schneider Contribution 1913–1931

France's contribution to the advancement of aviation has always been a great one, but never more so than in the early years between 1908 and 1913, when that nation's designer/aviators led the world. Around this period, France gave another major, if subtler, impetus to aviation in the form of sponsorship. One such French patron was Jacques Schneider, whose Schneider Trophy Cup was to contribute so much to the development of the aero-engine and that of the in-line, liquid-cooled variety in particular. Destined, sadly, to end in the recriminations of Britain's unsporting decision of 1931 to fly the Supermarine S.6B uncontested around the course, thus permanently gaining the Trophy for itself, this race was flown for the first time in April 1913 at Monaco, the then spiritual home of the seaplane.

Interrupted by the outbreak of war in 1914, the Schneider Trophy really came into its own with the 1923 event, which saw the ousting of the sportsman flier fraternity by the American armed service entries. From this point onwards, until the onset of the Great Depression in late 1929, the annual Schneider Trophy became a jousting ground for the pilots and machines of the world's leading air arms. Neither was it a pure coincidence that this change of participant 'ownership' heralded an era in which the floatplane was to dominate the realm of high speed flying. It needed the money and organisation that only the armed forces could provide, pushing engine and airframe development to the maximum. This said, there was one other reason seaplanes dominated the absolute world air speed listings during the years between 1925 and 1939 and this lay in the combination of aircraft development as it was then and the nature of water itself. Heavier than air machines, other than helicopters that barely existed at the start of this period, had always needed a certain amount of room for take-off and landing. While fighters and airliners alike clung to the stately biplane form, propelled by relatively modestly powered engines, all could continue happily operating in and out of grass airfields of reasonably manageable dimensions. However, one of the basic laws of physics predicates that to go faster, more power is needed and more power means more weight, not just in the engine, but in the fuel it consumes. Thus, by the early 1920s, the designer of high speed aircraft were beginning to confront the problematic issue of higher wing loadings. Because the wing loading of an aircraft predicates its flying speed and, hence, the stalling speed at which point

the machine quits flying, designers began to realise that given sufficient power, the higher they could 'grow' the wing loading, the higher speed they could achieve. The only problem with this was that it required progressively longer distances for take-off and landing. This space requirement put a very real constraint upon the landplane designers, who would have to come up with things like slats and flaps before progressing, while the waterborne

aircraft designer faced no such hindrance. After all, finding a patch of water three or so miles long was not the real estate problem faced by the landplane producer. Thus, by the late 1920s, the Schneider entries, with their unprecedented wing loadings were taking up to a mile and a half to 'unstick', but once aloft could more usefully employ the vast amounts of horsepower they carried.

With its contra-rotating propellers garlanded in victor's laurels, the **Macchi MC.72** and its proud pilot, Warrant Officer Francesco Agello, pose for photographers after completing their 23 October 1934 absolute world air speed record flight. Their record speed of 440.681mph still stands today and is likely to remain in perpetuity within the class it was set, namely propeller-driven floatplanes. (Italian Air Ministry)

Above Maurice Prevost is seen here sitting in the aft cockpit of the 160hp Gnome engined **Deperdussin** that he flew to victory in the first of the Schneider Trophy races. Held at Monaco during the period 3 to 6 April 1913, Prevost's winning speed was 45.75mph after having reflown a marker to satisfy the judges. Less well known is the fact that Prevost's race no. 19 had originally attired a much sleeker Deperdussin single seater, similar to the one in which he was to win the James Gordon Bennett Cup later in the year. Unfortunately for him, Prevost was compelled to race his standby machine, when the sleeker machine's double-banked rotary proved troublesome. (US National Archives)

The nimble looking **Sopwith Tabloid** with its Australian pilot, C. Howard Pixton, sitting nonchalantly on the lower wing leading edge. Carrying the race no. 3, the Tabloid, powered by a 100hp Gnome rotary bested three higher powered machines to win the 14 April 1914 Schneider Trophy, with a speed of 86.78mph. Consisting of a 28 lap race totalling 174 miles, the event was once again held in Monaco. Not content with winning, Pixton went on to fly another two laps, thereby setting a new world seaplane speed record of 86.6mph over a 300 kilometre, or 186.41 mile closed circuit course. (Hawker Siddeley)

Above Powered by a 275hp Hispano-Suiza 8Fb-42, this smoothly contoured **Nieuport 29C-1** was a modified, float-equipped variant of the Nieuport 29 single seat fighter, the major change being the reduction of 5 feet 9 inches in wingspan, taking out one bay of interplane struts. These refinements were estimated to add 12.5mph to the aircraft's top level speed, bringing it to 155.5mph. Two of these racers were produced for the 1919 Schneider Trophy and were issued with the race nos. 2 and 4. Unfortunately, both machines suffered mishaps that prevented their taking part in the event, no. 2, seen here, being totally destroyed. Happily, its Nieuport pilot, Jean Casale, survived.

Based on the company's N.1B Baby of 1918, the **Supermarine Sea Lion I** entry for the 1919 Schneider Trophy used far more power in the form of a the 450hp Napier Lion. Pre-race trials with the machines indicated a top level speed in excess of 140mph, but all was to little avail when the aircraft struck flotsam, holed its hull and sank during the fog-bound race that ended in total confusion. Happily, the basic Sea Lion design, with

the same engine, but known as the Sea Lion II and registered G-EBAH, race no. 1, went on to win the 1922 Schneider Trophy held at Naples, Italy, with a speed of 145.721mph. (Vickers)

The sole **Avro 539A** at Bournemouth preparing for the 10 September 1919 Schneider Trophy race. Built in a hurry for the race, the 240hp Siddeley Puma engined single seater first flew on 29 August 1919. Damaged during trials on 3 September, the opportunity was seized to increase both fin and rudder area, hence, the 'A' suffix to its designation. As it was, this effort was totally wasted as that year's race was declared void through a combination of sea fog and monumental organisational incompetence. Few performance details of the machine have survived. (Avro)

Below Two **Latham L-1s**, F-ATAM and F-ESEJ, seen here, were built as backups for the two CAMS 38s upon which France's main hopes rested. More robust than the CAMS, the Latham L-1s were fitted with twin 400hp Lorraine Dietrich engines mounted back-to-back above the fuselage to screen their propellers as much as possible from spray. Dogged by bad luck, the first L-1 was badly damaged while being off-loaded at Southampton and unable to race. The second machine fared little better, failing to complete the qualifying trials as a result of an engine magneto breakdown.

Above right Rebuilt from parts of the two **Navy-Wright NW-1** sesquiplanes, or one and a half wingers, discussed in the previous chapter, the sole float-equipped **NW-2**, Bu Aer A6544, was now powered by a 700hp Wright T-3 and fitted with Curtiss type wing surface radiators. Shipped to England for the 1923 Schneider Trophy race, as part of the impressive US Navy team, it was allocated the race no. 5. Regrettably, the NW-2, which wore the most powerful engine of all that year's entrants never got to show its capability, as its propeller broke up while being flight tested,, severely damaging the floats in the process. While its pilot, Lt. A. W. Gorton, succeeded in getting the machine down safely, the weakened floats collapsed on alighting and the aircraft sank shortly after Gorton had climbed, uninjured, from the cockpit. Interestingly, brief trials flown at the US Navy's Anacostia Flight Test Centre had indicated the NW-2 of being capable of more than 176mph, very close to that year's winning speed of 177.38mph, set by another US Navy pilot. (US Navy)

Overleaf Few pilots were to leave such an indelible mark on the annals of 20th-century aviation as **James Harold 'Jimmy' Doolittle**. Born in 1896, Doolitle, seen here in 1932, joined the US Army in 1917, gaining his wings in March 1918. At this time, Doolittle was mixing his flight instructor's duty with boxing for the Army. He became the first man to fly across the US in less than a day, when, on 4 September 1922, he crossed from Pablo Beach, Florida, to San Diego, California, in a DH 4, making one stop at Kelly Field, Texas and taking an overall 21 hours 20 minutes. Always gifted with a keen mind, Doolittle studied at the Massachusetts Institute of Technology. As a result, 'Jimmy' Doolittle, accomplished aerobatic pilot, also became a Doctor of Aeronautics and one of the first Americans to hold this highest of qualifications. In 1928, Doolittle started research into instrument flying, culminating, on 24 September 1929, with him flying a Consolidated NY-2 trainer solo and under a blind flying hood to point out advances achieved. As he approached the age of 33, and still only a lowly first lieutenant, Doolittle succumbed to the lure of commerce and resigned his Army commission to join Shell Petroleum's newly formed St Louis-based Aviation Department as its manager on 15 February 1930. There followed a brief, but

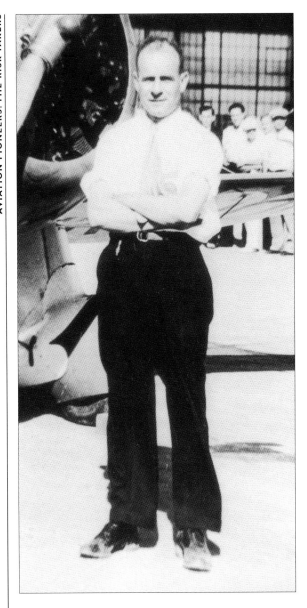

Seen here prior to having it race no. 3 applied, is the **Curtiss R3C-2** flown by US Army Lt. J. H. 'Jimmy' Doolittle in the Baltimore-based 1925 Schneider Trophy held on 26 October. Doolittle won the race with a speed of 232.573mph, well ahead of the rest of the two other race finishing aircraft, both of which were European. Power for the R3C-2 was the 619hp Curtiss V-1400. Both US Navy R3C-2s retired on the seventh lap. (US Air Force)

Wearing its 1925 Schneider Trophy race no. 7, the 500hp Curtiss D-12A powered **Macchi M.33** took third place in the hands of Giovanni de Briganti, one of Macchi's test pilots. Briganti's speed was 168.444mph. A second M.33, to have been flown by Ricardo Morselli, failed to start as a result of ignition problems. The two M.33s not only carried the least powerful engines, they were also the oldest and probably most used engines, having been bought by the Italian Government in 1924 and extensively tested by Fiat prior to being donated to Macchi as the government's sole contribution in support of the Italian team.

brilliant two or more years as a Shell-paid racing pilot, during which time he established a world air speed record for landplanes flying a treacherous machine, the Gee Bee Super Sportster R. Wisely, after the Super Sportster, Doolittle turned to flying of a less life threatening nature, until, with war clouds forming over Europe, he rejoined the US Army Air Corps in 1940. Back in uniform, Doolittle showed his planning skills and bravery simultaneously, with his April 1942 raid on Tokyo. Leading this raid, Doolittle and his North American B-25 medium bomber crews took off from the deck of the USS Hornet on a one-way mission in which the bombing run must have been the easy part! By the end of the war, Doolittle was commanding the mighty US 8th Air Force. Retiring from active duty shortly there-after, Dr Doolittle was elected Chairman of the US Air Force's Scientific Advisory Committee on its formation in 1947, a post he held in parallel with equally pivotal roles in Shell and TRW. Small, perhaps, in stature, 'Jimmy' Doolittle, who died in 1993, was great in both mind and spirit. (US Air Force)

The handsome **Curtiss R3C-4**, race no. 4 in the 1926 Schneider Trophy, was flown by US navy Lt. George Cuddihy. Considered America's best prospect following the pre-race crash of the 700hp Packard powered R3C-3, Cuddihy's prospects were smashed as a result of a fuel pump failure starving his 700hp Curtiss V-1570, which forced him out on the seventh and last lap. This said, there is

no reason to believe that either of the Curtiss biplanes could have ever outpaced the formidable Macchi M.39. (US Navy)

and the 'de-bugging' of problems. (Italian Air Ministry)

Winning combination, Major M. de Bernardi and his **Macchi M.39**, MM76, race no. 5, winner of the 1926 Schneider Trophy held on 13 November at Hampton Roads, Virginia. De Bernardi's speed of 246.5mph was 15.1mph better than of the second placed Curtiss R3C-2. In all, five of these M.39 were to be built, including two lower powered trainers with greater wingspan and area. A second Macchi M.39, flown by Lt. Bacula, was placed third with a speed of 218.006mph. A few days later, on 17 November, de Bernardi, while still in Virginia, went on to set a new world absolute speed record of 258.873mph. Worthy of comment is the fact that the first flight of the M.39 took place on 6 July 1926, providing the aircraft with one of the longest lead times to the race date yet. This, of course, meant more time for flight testing

Beauty and danger often seemed to go together in the 1920s as exemplified by the sole **Supermarine S.4**, built for the 1925 Schneider Trophy. First flown on 24 August 1925 and powered by a 700hp Napier Lion Special, the S.4 was exceptionally clean with fully cantilevered, or externally unbraced wings and tailplane. Early flight testing had thrown up indications of excessive vibration in the rolling axis at high speed, this same phenomena recurring during the qualifying flight over Chesapeake Bay on 23 October. However, the effect was so severe this time that the pilot, Henri Biard, lost control and crashed into the bay Happily, Biard survived the incident, attributed to the onset of high speed wing flutter. The only marks ever carried by the S.4 was the race no. 4 as it crashed before it could be bought by the Air Ministry. (Vickers)

N219, the first of the three **Supermarine S.5s** to be built. Its sister, N220 went on to win the 1927 Schneider trophy, while, sadly, the last of the trio, N221, was to dive into the sea killing its pilot, Flt. Lt. Kinkead, on 28 March 1928, while attempting to set a new absolute world air speed record. First flown on 27 June 1927, N220 was fitted with a 900hp direct drive Napier Lion VIIA, while the other two had 875hp geared Lion VIIBs. At Venice, on 26 September, the British were represented by the RAF's recently formed High Speed Flight with no less than seven aircraft comprising all three S.5s, three Gloster IVs and the Short-Bristol Crusader, of which three, two S.5s, N220, race no. 4, N219, race no. 6 and Gloster IVB, N223, race no. 1 actually participated. S.5, N220, flown by Flt. Lt. S. N. Webster, went on to win with a speed of 281.65mph. S.5, N219, flown by Flt. Lt. O. E. Worsley, came second at 273.07mph, while the Gloster IVB and 2 Macchi M.52s retired. Later, on 4 November 1928, S.5, N220, was to set a new absolute world speed record of 319.57mph. (Vickers)

Above right Three of these exquisitely styled **Gloster IV** floatplanes were produced for the 1927 Schneider Trophy. All were slightly different, the first, N224 was the IV with greater wing area than the others, while IVA, N222, and VIB, N222, employed a 875hp geared Napier Lion VIIB and 900hp direct drive Lion VIIA, respectively. Only the Gloster IVB competed, wearing the race no. 1. Flown by Flt. Lt. S. M. Kinkead, the machine retired on the sixth lap with propeller problems. Seen here is the IVA, N222. (Gloster)

Opposite top One of the three **Macchi M.52s** that participated unsuccessfully in the 1927 Venice-based Schneider Trophy held on 26 September. Both the airframe and engine were, in essence, simple improvements of the previous year's winner, the M.52 using a 1,000 hp Fiat AS3. First flown in early August 1927, the highest speed recorded by a M.52 was 318.623mph, achieved when establishing a new absolute world air speed mark on 30 March 1928, with Major de Bernardi at the controls. (Italian Air Ministry)

Below Initiated in the spring of 1926, the **Short-Bristol Crusader's** primary purpose was to provide a high speed development mount for Bristol's new 808hp Mercury I radial, although it was a logical candidate to be inducted into the RAF High Speed Flight, formed in October 1926, thus explaining its appearance at Venice for the 1927 Schneider Trophy. First flown in the early summer of 1927, early engine cooling problems associated with the use of individual cylinder fairings promised to be eradicated by their replacement with a Townend Ring. However. this was yet to be fitted when the sole example, N226, was shipped to Italy. On 11 September, Flt. Lt. H. M. Schofield took the machine out for a post-reassembly check flight. Unbeknown to him. one of the riggers had inadvertently crossed the aileron controls and when a wing dropped just prior to lift-off, Schofield's reaction only increased the roll rate, causing a 150mph roll-cum-cartwheel into the waters of the Lido, from which a wet Schofield emerged limp and bedraggled, but basically sound of limb. (Shorts)

Below and overleaf Two views of the ill-fated **Savoia Marchetti S.65** of 1929. Powered by two 1,000hp, tandem-mounted Isota-Fraschini I-500s housed in the central nacelle that barely left room to squeeze a small pilot in between, the overall airframe design could be described as minimalist. Thus the wings and nacelle were attached to the tail by two slim booms to minimise weight and drag. The S.65's estimated top level speed was 348mph, but protracted engine related problem prevented the machine from participating in the 1929 Schneider Trophy at Calshot. Testing of the S.65 continued, with Tommaso Dal Molin as the only pilot capable of squeezing into to its tiny cockpit. On 18 January 1930, the S.65 was flying at high speed over Lake Garda at a height of around 65 feet, when for reasons unknown, it dived into the lake, killing Dal Molin as it broke up. (Italian Air Ministry)

If the design of the S.65 was unusual, that of the one-off, semi-submersible **Piaggio-Pegna Pc 7** almost defies description. The brainchild of engineer Giovanni Pegna, an early advocate of the hydrofoil, the Pc 7 used hydrofoils rather than floats. Like the later Convair XF2Y-1 Seadart, this choice imposed just too many mechanical and handling problems, most important of which was to provide a pilot-managed system of clutches to permit the engine to drive a rear-mounted water propeller in order to get the whole craft moving and up onto its hydrofoils, before reclutching the engine to drive the normal, forward-mounted airscrew. It was this clutching system that could never be made to work satisfactorily. (Piaggio)

Designed by the US Navy Aircraft Factory, the **Williams Mercury floatplane** was to have been a contender for the 1929 Schneider Trophy, but never even left its homeland as a result of a lack of money and support. Based on the 1927 Kirkham-Williams Biplane racer, work on the Williams Mercury was started in September 1928, with its owner, Alfred 'Al' Williams financing its construction by public donation under the aegis of the Mercury Foundation. Costs were cut wherever possible, the earlier machine's engine, a 1,250hp Packard X-2775 being used. Completed in early August 1929 at a cost of $175,000, initial attempts to 'unstick' the machine failed and when it eventually flew on 18 August it became immediately apparent that the aircraft was both underpowered and overweight by about 400lb. Packard offered 'Al' Williams a new 1,500hp engine, but by this time the US

Navy had withdrawn its offer to ship the racer to England and the whole project crumbled. It was these events and the rumpus over the Mercury Foundation that triggered Williams' leaving and lasting resentment of the US Navy. (US National Archives)

Supermarine S.6, N247, race no. 2 and winner of the Solent-based 1929 Schneider Trophy. First flown on 10 August 1929, the S.6, of which two were built, was the fruit of the newly founded collaboration between Supermarine and Rolls-Royce, using the 1,900hp Rolls-Royce Type R. Flown on 7 September in bright, sunny conditions, the 1929 event again went in Britain's favour, with N247, flown by Flg. Off. H. R. D. Waghorn, showing a clean pair of heels to its nearest rival, Dal Molin's Macchi M.52, their speeds being 328.629mph and 284.2mph, respectively. The second S.6, N248, race no. 8, flown by Flg. Off. Richard Atcherly recorded 325.54mph, but was disqualified for cutting a course marker. Both S.6s were brought up to S.6A standard in the spring of 1931, but, tragically, N247 was to be lost on 18 August that year, as a result of mishandling on take-off, tricky at the best of times, that led to the death of its pilot, Lt. J. Brinton, RN. By now, it should be noted, with the major jump in engine power, both the task of the designer and the pilot was calling for great skill and care. High speed flutter needed the designers' attention as did the aircraft's water handling. This involved putting far more fuel into one float, which also served as the fuel tanks, than in the other in order to counteract the tremendous engine/airscrew torque. From the pilot's aspect, take-off involved off-setting the initial heading, again to compensate for torque, along with maintaining full back pressure on the joystick until well airborne. Thus, every 'unstick' was made in a dangerous semi-stalled attitude even with miles of open water available. (Vickers)

Bottom right Two of the sleek **Gloster VIs** were built for the 1929 Schneider Trophy, N249, seen here, and N250. The engine selected for these machines was the 1,320hp supercharged Napier Lion VIID. Sadly for both Gloster and Napier, this engine proved incapable of being run at full throttle under race conditions, thus forcing both aircraft to withdraw from the race. A part of the problem was the lack of time available to resolve engine-related problems, as the Gloster IV's first flight was only made on 25 August, two weeks prior to race day. By way of part recompense, N249 did manage to set a new absolute world air speed record of 336.3mph on 10 September 1929, the pilot was Flt. Lt. G. H. Stainforth. (Gloster)

Supermarine S.6B, S1596, the second of the pair of S.6Bs built, both with Rolls-Royce Type R engines boosted to give 2,300hp. According to the designer, R. J. Mitchell, the biggest problem was finding some remaining external surface upon which to place the additional heat-exchanging elements necessary to cope with the increased engine power. Initial attempts to fly in late July 1931, saw the S.6B chasing its tail in circles across the water, a result of the greater engine torque. This problem was eventually overcome by using a smaller diameter airscrew and increasing the fuel loading assymetry. Thus, on 13 September 1931, S1595, race no. 1, piloted by Flt. Lt. John Boothman, flew, unopposed, to give Britain the Schneider Trophy once and for all, with a speed of 340.08mph. Just over two weeks later, on 29 September, Flt. Lt.

G. H. Stainforth flew S1595 to set a new absolute world air speed record of 407.5mph. (Vickers)

Above First flown in July 1931, five of these truly impressive **Macchi MC.72s** were built in 1931–1932, three in time for the September 1931 Schneider Trophy, representing a concerted Italian Government-backed attempt to retrieve the nation's aeronautical prestige. As with all of these racers, the key to their success lay with the engine, which in the case of the MC.72 was a 3,100hp Fiat AS6, a unit that actually comprised of two Fiat AS5 coupled in tandem, with each driving its own two-bladed airscrew in contra-rotating fashion. In the event, 'teething troubles' with these extremely complicated engines kept the Italians from flying in what was to be the final Schneider Trophy. However, despite this early setback, the MC.72 was to prove unstoppable as a record setter, hitting 423.8mph in April 1933, before going on to set a new absolute world air speed record of 440.681mph on 23 October 1934. Flown by Warrant Officer Francesco Agello, this record was to stand for nearly five and a half years, at a time when previous records were lucky to last a matter of months. Technically, it is interesting to compare the British and Italian approaches to getting the necessary engine power, for while more powerful in terms of output, the Fiat AS6 was far heavier and more complex that the Rolls-Royce Type R, relegating it to the ranks of the one-off novelty, whereas the Type R was to father two illustrious lines of engines in the shape of the Merlin and Griffon. (Italian Air Ministry)

Air Racing's Golden Era, 1929-1940

While the body of this chapter is necessarily devoted to the spectacle and impact of air racing in the **US** and in particular that country's premier event, the **US** Nationals, glimpses of other aspects are interlaced to add perspective. High altitude flying is one such area, which, on the evidence, received scant attention from other than the Italian and British governments as far as heavier-than-air flying was concerned. Whilst the **US** put most of its high altitude efforts into helium ballooning. Thus, in the **US** much of the early initiative leading to the emergence of the modern, pressurised airliner, capable of overflying most storm weather conditions, appears to have come primarily from the vision of one man, Wiley Post. even if he could only afford to part pressurise himself, rather than his aircraft.

Another aspect of this era often overlooked is the impact of styling on aircraft design, taking the fast, but infamous, pilot-killing **Gee Bee Super Sportster R** as a prime example. As becomes clear later in this section, this machine, the brainchild of designer Robert L. Hall, was not only rotund in the extreme, it was the epitome of the theory that given enough power, anything could be made to fly. As first flown it had no fin and, to make matters worse, its short, fat fuselage provided virtually no keel area, making it extremely unstable to fly, as Russell Boardman discovered during his brief first flight in the machine. Quite how Boardman couched his criticism of Hall's design efforts are not recorded, but the racer promptly grew a small, but distinct fin prior to its next flight. However, curing the racer's overall instability problems and vicious stall would have required a total re-design and so it remained in service, to be flown at the risk of the pilot's very life. While the **Gee Bee Rs** may have been the prime examples, they were far from the only instances where style prevailed over common sense. In Britain, the De Havilland **DH 84 Dragon**'s very practical blunt wingtips were to be replaced by very pointed ones on subsequent models, such as the **DH 86**, **DH 88 Comet** and **DH 89 Dragon Rapide**. Fine as these wingtips looked from an artistic vantage, they induced low speed handling problems galore for their pilots. As Hubert Broad, the famous freelance test pilot of that period pointed out, they not only provided a vicious stall, they induced random wing dropping. Broad wanted no part of such developments and parted ways with the De Havilland company, for whom he had often test flown prototypes.

Seen here is the second of five **Travel Air Model Rs** built, R614K, powered by a neatly-cowled 400hp supercharged Wright R-975-9 Whirlwind. Winner of the 'Free-for-All' race that concluded the 1929 US Nationals, N614K, piloted by sportsman flier 'Doug' Davis, clocked 194.9mph, romping home 8mph ahead of its nearest rival, a US Army Curtiss P-3A. Thus on 2 September 1929, a civilian racer, the first of a new breed was to shatter the former dominance of the Army and Navy fighters in US air racing. (Beech)

R614K

#1475

N613K, the first of the five **Travel Air Model Rs** that made their debut in the summer of 1929, in time for that year's US Nationals, held at Cleveland, Ohio, between 24 August and 2 September. Rarely seen, as here, in its initial form with a 250hp Chevrolair. Sadly, this brand-new 6-cylinder in-line engine from the Chevrolet brothers clearly needed more development work, forcing N613K, piloted by 'Doug' Davis to limp in at 113.38mph in an early event. Re-engined with a Townsend ringed 300hp Wright Whirlwind, Florence 'Poncho' Barnes flew N613K to set a new woman's air speed record of 196.19mph on 5 August 1930, at Glendale, California. (Beech)

Below, above right and right Long distance flying seemed to occupy the minds of the military as much as the individual during this era, the Italian Air Force being, perhaps, the most active of all in this area. Mostly, they used standard production aircraft flown in large numbers to far off places, but, in the instance of the **Savoia-Marchetti S.64**, they went to the trouble of building two of these dedicated record setters. Powered by a single, pylon mounted 520hp Fiat A22T pusher engine, the S.64 used many of the S.55 flying boat's components. Most of both S.64's flying was carried was carried out by **Lt. Col. Umberto Maddalena**, seen here on the left and **Lt. Fausto Cecconi**. Flying the first S.64, the pair reached Brazil, where the machine was damaged beyond economic repair on landing. Later, in the second machine, they set a new world closed circuit distance record of 5,088.275 miles between 30 May and 2 July 1930. This non-stop flight kept the two airmen aloft for 67 hours 13 minutes. Regrettably, both men were to be killed in the S.64 shortly afterwards, when the machine crashed following an in-flight fire. The photo above right shows the special ramped runway built to help the fuel-laden S.64 on take-off. A similar ramp was built at the US Army Air Force's Wright Field in early 1942 to aid the Boeing B-29's development. (Italian Air Ministry)

Above right **Wiley Post's** winning of the 1930 US Nationals' Los Angeles to Chicago race may have propelled him to prominence, but for Post himself, it represented the culmination of many flying hours experience and a formidable personal determination. Born on 22 November 1898, Post had become a barnstorming parachutist in 1924, receiving some basic pilot training in the process. As barnstorming did not pay much, Post turned to work as an oil rigger, where in 1926 he was to lose his left eye. Post promptly used part of his compensation to buy a surplus Curtiss JN, while much of the remainder was spent on his elopement and marriage in 1927. The 1930 Nationals win eased his path considerably, allowing him to make two round-the-world flights in 1931 and 1933. In the wake of these, Post showed his scientific vision by having his Lockheed Vega, the famed 'Winnie Mae', stripped out and given a jettisonable landing gear for extra lightness. In parallel with the aircraft weight reduction, Post approached the Goodrich company to produce a partial pressure suit for him. Thus equipped, Post embarked on a number of high altitude flights between early September 1934 and April 1935. Two of these deserve special mention. On one occasion, without government support, Post reached a height of 48,000 feet, while on another flight, between Burbank, California, and Cleveland, Ohio, and, cruising at 30,000 feet, he achieved an over the ground speed of 279mph. As this 15 March 1935 flight was made at an average

speed of 99mph faster than the top level speed of a late model Vega, Post had clearly demonstrated the advantages of riding the high altitude jetstreams. On 15 August 1935, Wiley Post and his friend, the famous American comedian, Will Rogers, were killed when Post's recently acquired Lockheed Orion floatplane crashed in Alaska, ironically on the day the US Congress approved $25,000 to purchase 'Winnie Mae' for the nation. (Lockheed)

Unquestionably, **Lockheed 5C Vega**, NR105W, 'Winnie Mae', seen here with Wiley Post, was the most famous of all the 129 Vegas originally built. Completed in June 1930, Post used this 450hp Pratt & Whitney Wasp C1-powered machine on his late-August 1,760 miles dash from Los Angeles to Chicago in

9 hours 9 minutes, 4 seconds at the start of that year's US Nationals. Later, used by Post on two round-the-world flights, first accompanied by Harold Gatty in June-July 1931 and then solo in July 1933: this latter flight taking 7 days, 18 hours, 49 minutes. The view of man and machine shown here is at the start of Post's high altitude research flying in September 1934, as it shows the Vega yet to be fitted with its central belly skid for landing following the jettisoning of its main wheels. Pictures of Post wearing the eye patch only date from this period, as flight at such heights caused his glass eye to discomfort him. (Lockheed)

The **Wedell-William Special**, NR635V, the extremely rare James 'Jimmy' Wedell designed racer of 1930. Seen here in its later form, fitted with a 535hp Pratt & Whitney Wasp Jr, the initial engine had been a 110hp High Drive Ensign in-line. (US Air Force Museum)

The sole **Curtiss XF6C-6**, Bu Aer A7147, had been returned to the Curtiss plant in June 1930 for drastic modifications in preparation for that year's US Nationals and the Thompson Trophy in particular. Previously the 20th of 35 Curtiss F6C-3 biplanes, the XF6C-6 retained its upper wing, retrofitted with Curtiss surface type radiators, the whole lower wing was deleted. Given a special 770hp Curtiss V-1570 Conqueror, the XF6C-6 was generally considered unbeatable. Flown by US Marine Corps Capt. Arthur Page in the Thompson, the machine was showing a clean pair of heels to the rest of the field, averaging 219mph during the first 16 laps. Suddenly, on the 17th lap, the big Navy racer failed to make a pylon turn, arced up, before inverting into a dive and crashing. Overcome with exhaust fumes that had leaked into the cockpit,

Capt. Page had managed to switch off the ignition prior to impact, but, sadly, died of his injuries the next day. (US Navy)

Completed an hour or so before the start of the 1930 Thompson Trophy in which it was to race on 1 September, the **Laird Solution**, NR10538, had only time for a 10 minute air test before departing to the nearby race site at Curtiss-Reynolds Field, Chicago. On this occasion, the test-cum-race pilot was airline captain, Charles 'Speed' Holman, who, it was said, flew the machine with some caution. Despite his understandable total lack of familiarity with this potent 470hp Pratt & Whitney engined biplane, Holman still managed an outright win with a speed of 201.91mph after the previously leading Curtiss XF6C-6 had crashed. (US Air Force)

Built around a borrowed 98hp Wright-built DH Gipsy I, the diminutive **Howard DGA 3**, NR2Y, 'Pete' romped home at 162.8mph to take third place in the 20-lap, 100-mile 1930 Thompson following first- and second- place holders flying with 470hp and 400hp, respectively. The pilot of 'Pete', race no. 37, was the 26-year-old Benjamin 'Ben' Odell Howard, airline pilot and 'Pete's' co-designer with the 18-year-old Gordon Israel. First flown in July 1930, 'Pete's' designers went on to produce the 1933 Thompson third-placed DGA 4 'Mike'. the DGA 5 'Ike' and the legendary 1935 Thompson winning DGA 6 'Mr Mulligan'. DGA, incidentally, stood for 'Damn Good Airplane'. (US Air Force)

Above The career of the sole **Vickers Vespa VII** is an extremely convoluted saga that ended in a largely unsung triumph. First flown in September 1925, as the sole Vespa I, G-EBLD, the machine was fitted with metal wings to become the Vespa II, serving as the prototype for the six Bolivian Vespa IIIs, plus the four of each of the Vespa IVs and Vs sold to Ireland. Meanwhile, in January 1931, the original G-EBLD turned up, this time modified into Mk. VI form and with the new registration, G-ABIL. Following an unfruitful demonstration in China, the machine returned to Britain to become the Mk. VII when fitted with a 525hp supercharged Bristol Pegasus S. In this guise, Cyril Uwins of Bristol took the aircraft to 43.976 feet on 16 September 1931, to set a new world altitude record. (Vickers)

The **Laird Super Solution**, NR12048, of Shell Aviation. Powered by a 535hp Pratt & Whitney R-985 Wasp Jr., the machine was entered for the brand new 1931 gruelling cross-country Bendix Trophy. Starting from Burbank, California, at dawn on 4 September 'Jimmy' Doolittle, competing against three Lockheed monoplanes (two Orions and an Altair), covered the 2,043 mile event at a speed of 223.038mph to win it. However, not content, Doolittle did his own refuelling without leaving the cockpit and promptly set off, heading for Newark, New Jersey. 'Jimmy' touched down at Newark after leaving Burbank 11 hours, 16 minutes, 10 seconds previously setting a new west-to-east crossing record, nearly 1 hour, 9 minutes faster than the previous best time put up by Frank Hawks in his Texaco-owned Travel Air Model R. Incidentally, the Super Solution's 1931 racing no. 400 just happened to be that of Shell Aviation's latest product line and was, somewhat confusingly, also applied to Shell Aviation Travel Air Model R. (US National Archives)

The sole **Gee Bee Super Sportster Model Z**, NR77V, with a justifiably pleased looking designer/pilot Robert L. 'Bob' Hall standing in its cockpit after winning the General Tyre Trophy in the 1931 US Nationals, with a speed of 189.545mph. Rolled out of the Granville Brothers' plant at Springfield, Massachusetts, on 22 August, just seven days ahead of the Nationals, NR77V was fitted with a 535hp Pratt & Whitney Wasp Jr. Following the Hall win, NR77V went on to win that years Shell Oil Speed Dash at 267.342mph, rounding off by winning the 1931 Thompson Trophy with a speed of 236.239mph, beating the second place Wedell Williams '44' by over 8mph. On both of these later flights, NR77V was piloted by owner Lowell Bayles. (Grumman)

Lowell Bayles standing in front of the **Gee Bee Super Sportster Model R** shortly before what was to be a fatal attempt to set a new world landplane speed record. On 30 November 1931, NR77V, still wearing its original 535hp Wasp Jr. had been coaxed to reach 284.5mph in a straight line dash and now, fitted with a 700hp Pratt & Whitney Wasp at the beginning of December, was expected to readily exceed the 300mph mark. On 5 December, Bayles lifted NR77V in the air for the record attempt, but lost control at high speed and low level to impact and cartwheel to a fiery demise. As the aircraft's fuel cap was discovered some distance back from the crash site, it was thought that this had smashed through the windscreen to cause the disaster. (Granville Brothers)

Comper Gipsy Swift, G-ABWW, the second of only two high speed Swifts built for the 1932 King's Cup. Owned by the Prince of Wales, later Edward VIII, the machine was flown by Flt. Lt. E. H. Fielden, seen here executing a text book three point landing. Painted in purple and blue with silver trim, these colours were later adopted by the RAF's Royal Flight that Fielden would command. Fielden was placed second in the 1932 event, the Swift averaging 155.75mph on its 120hp DH Gipsy III. Six years later,

G-ABWW went on to win the 4 June, 1938, Hatfield to Ronaldsway, Isle of Man, air race with a speed of 159.5mph.

A study in silver, this Yugoslavian **Hawker Fury I**, flown by Capt. Stinic of the Yugoslav Air Force, took the overall winner's position in the July 1932 annual Zurich International Military Aircraft Meeting, with a speed of 201mph. The Yugoslavs had ordered six Furies in the early part of 1931, deliveries of which had commenced in the late spring of that year, in parallel with initial deliveries to the RAF. Power for the Fury I was provided by a 480hp supercharged Rolls-Royce Kestrel IS. (Cowin Collection)

Opposite top A natural showman, the colourful **Roscoe Turner** was born in 1895 and is seen here in 1932 with his mascot, Gilmore, his pet lion cub and his main source of income at the time. Turner had been taught parachuting as part of his US Army training as a balloonist after he had joined up in 1917. Unfortunately, for Turner both the war and his Army career ended before he could achieve his ambition of gaining his pilot's wings. Undaunted, Turner put his service gratuity into a flying circus partnership and was taught to fly in 1921 by his pilot

partner. Always fastidious in his appearance, Turner designed his own uniform and bestowed upon himself the title 'Colonel'. Turner spent much of the 1920s and early 1930s living beyond his means and dodging writ servers and debt collectors with equal facility. Using his real gift for self-promotion, Turner approached the Los Angeles-based Gilmore Oil Company in 1930 with his 'Gilmore the lion' idea as a promotion. Gilmore liked the idea and bought the used Lockheed Air Express, NC3057, which forms the backdrop to this picture, for him to fly. Shortly afterwards, in May 1930, after one failed attempt, Turner flew this machine west-to-east across the US in 18 hours, 42 minutes, 54 seconds to set a new record time. Despite his 'comic opera uniform' and 'live-now, pay-later' philosophy, Turner was a more than competent pilot going on to become the only man to win the coveted Thompson Trophy no less than three times: in 1934, 1938 and 1939. Sometimes overlooked was Turner's creditable third, place flying a Boeing 247D, in the McPherson Robinson England to Australia air race of October 1934. (Lockheed)

James R. 'Jimmy' Wedell sits in his 550hp Pratt & Whitney Wasp Jr. engined **Wedell-Williams**, NR278V, which carries the 1932 US Nationals race no. 44. Entered for both the opening Bendix Trophy and the closing Thompson, 'Jimmy' Wedell took second place in both races with speeds of 232mph and 242.469mph, respectively. Winner of that year's Bendix long distance event was James Haizlip in a similar Wedell-Williams, who clocked 245mph, before continuing on to set a new west-to-east US crossing record of 10 hours 19 minutes to cover the 2,450 miles between Burbank, Califonia and Floyd Bennett Field, New York. (US Air Force)

Gilmore Oil's **Wedell-Williams**, NR61Y, 1932 US Nationals' race no. 121, seen here at Burbank in company with Roscoe Turner's other mount, Lockheed Air Express, NC3057. Shown

here in its original form, the Gilmore Wedell-Williams wore an overall cream finish with red trim. Turner brought '121' into third place in that year's Bendix Trophy, with a speed of 226mph, with the same design taking first and second places in the event, being flown by James Haizlip and James Wedell, respectively, their speeds being 245mph and 232mph. (Lockheed)

Flown initially on 14 November 1928, the first of the two **Fairey Postal**, or Long Range, Monoplanes built failed to set any new distance records before crashing on 16 December 1929, killing its two pilots, Sdn. Ldr. A. G. Jones-Williams and Flt. Lt. N. H. Jenkins. The second machine, K1991, seen here, made its maiden flight on 30 June 1931, embarking on a protracted series of proving flights. At dawn on 6 February 1933, K1991 departed Cranwell, Lincolnshire, landing at Walvis Bay, South West Africa, some 57 hours, 25 minutes later and covering a new world record distance of 5,341 miles. The crew on this extended flight was Sdn. Ldr. O. R Gayford and Flt. Lt. G. E. Nicolette. Both Long Range Monoplanes were powered by a 570hp Napier Lion XIA, giving the machines a cruising speed of around 112mph. Still-air range was quoted as 5,500 miles. (Fairey Aviation)

Russell Boardman, owner/pilot, stands beside the first of the two **Gee Bee Super Sportster Model Rs**, NR2100, Seen here just prior to its first, brief flight of 13 August 1932, the lack of effective fin area made the aircraft extremely difficult to handle directionally and Boardman called for an increased fin area prior to making any more flights. (Granville Brothers)

Gee Bee Super Sportster Model R, NR2100, seen after additional fin area had been fitted and wearing its 1932 US Nationals race no. 11. As it transpired, Russell Boardman was prevented from flying the machine due to injury and a last minute scramble to find a pilot led to J. H 'Jimmy' Doolittle stepping in to fly it. Describing the Super Sportster Model R as 'the touchiest

plane I've ever been in', Doolittle, nonetheless managed to fly it into first place in that year's Shell Speed dash with a speed of 294.418mph and set a new world speed record for landplanes in the process. Not content with this, Doolittle went on to win that year's Thompson closing event at a speed of 252.686mph. This is where the two parted, Doolittle quitting air racing, while the two Model Rs and their descendants went on to specialise in pilot killing. (US National Archives)

Seen here is the first major rebuild of the **Gee Bee Super Sportster Model R**, created by marrying components from the two original aircraft. Initially, the Granville Brothers' enterprise had built two Model Rs, R-1, NR2100, with its 800hp Pratt & Whitney Wasp Sr and R-2, NR2101, powered by a 550hp Wasp Jr. R-1 had crashed, fatally injuring Russell Boardman on 1 July 1933, while competing in that year's 2,050 mile New York to Los Angeles Bendix Trophy. By coincidence, R-2 was also damaged at the same place and day, when ground looped at Indianapolis by Russell Thaw. Undeterred, the Granville Brothers took the wings of R-2, the fuselage and tail unit of R-1 now stretched by almost two feet and married them all to a 575hp Pratt & Whitney Hornet. Given the R-2's registration, NR2101 and the 1934 US Nationals race no. 7, as seen here, the hybrid was taxied into a ditch prior to the start of the races on 31 August. Incidentally, the initials 'I.F.' on the engine cowling stood for 'Intestinal Fortitude'. Rebuilt, once again, this time with a pair of wings that raised doubts in many minds, the resurrected machine was bought by Cecil Allen, a pilot with more ambition than money and entered for the 1935 Bendix. Sadly, the underfinanced Allen could not afford the fuel for pre-race testing and familiarisation. On 31 August, shortly after lifting-off from Burbank for Cleveland, Allen crashed and died. (US Air Force)

Above More attractively contoured than 'Ben' Howard's DGA 3, this second racer from the stables of Howard and Israel, their **DGA 4**, NR55Y, 'Mike' was powered by a 225hp Menasco B-6. Seen here with the 1932 US Nationals race no. 38 and flown by William Ong, 'Mike' secured two seconds, a fourth and two fifth places in various events that year. Things turned out better for 'Mike', however, in the 1935 US Nationals, when in the hands of Harold Neumann, 'Mike', retaining race no. 38, stormed home to win the three heat Greve Trophy with a aggregate speed of 212.716mph. (Al Menasco)

'Art' Chester's famed **Chester Special**, later known as Jeep, NR12930, seen here in its 1933 US Nationals guise with race no. 15, where it took no less than five prizes. Designed and built by Chester in his Glenview, Illinois, garage, the Chester Special had a wingspan of no more that 16 feet 8 inches. With its 1,150lb

gross weight, the wing loading was 24 lb/sq ft, making it a relatively 'hot ship' to handle. Powered by a 225hp Menasco C-4S, the name Jeep was adopted for the 1936 US Nationals, where the machine came third in the Greve Trophy at 225mph. (Al Menasco)

The modified **Caproni Ca 113**, with its pilot Cdt. Renato Donati lost in the crowd, after setting a new world altitude record for aeroplanes of 47,352 feet on 11 April 1934. This particular Ca 113 had been modified to take a 530hp Bristol Pegasus in place of its normal 370hp Piaggion Stella VII. (Italian Air Ministry)

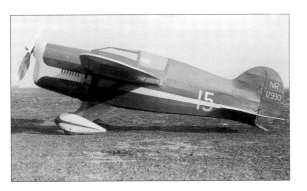

Overleaf A standard 75hp Pobjoy R-powered **Comper Swift**, G-ACML, wearing its 1934 King's Cup race no. 18, taxies out for the start of this 13-14 July event based at Hatfield, Hertfordshire. This machine, flown by Flt. Lt. R. P .P. Pope was unplaced on this occasion. The Pobjoy-engined version, of which 39 were

produced, had a top level speed of 140mph, along with a range of 380 miles at a cruising speed of 120mph. (via M. J Hooks)

Below Designed by Lawrence Brown around a 300hp Menasco C-6S, the **Brown B-2**, NR255Y 'Miss Los Angeles' was built for the 1934 US Nationals, to be held at Cleveland, Ohio. With a wingspan of 19 feet 3 inches, along with a gross weight of 1,299lb, the wing loading of 21.65lb/sq ft was eased by the employment of wing flaps. Carrying the race no. 33, 'Miss Los Angeles' took second place in the Thompson Trophy, with a

speed of 214.929mph when flown by Roy Minor. Not bad for a machine that had required repairs after a landing 'nose over' earlier in the races. Much modified over the next five years, the Brown B-2 was finally destroyed during the 1939 US Nationals' Greves Trophy. As seen here, the aircraft's designer, Lawrence Brown is on the left, next is A. J. Menasco, the engine maker, while pilot Roy Minor occupies the cockpit. (Al Menasco)

Opposite top Seen here in its latter-day Portuguese marking, CS-AAJ, 'Salazar', this **De Havilland DH 88 Comet** was, in fact,

the first of five examples built. It started life as G-ACSP, first flown on 8 September, 1934. Powered by two 230hp DH Gipsy Sixs and built for the MacPherson Robertson England-to-Australia air race of October 1934, this machine failed to finish, but DH 88, G-ACSS, 'Grosvenor House' finished first, with a an overall time of 70 hours 54 minutes 18 seconds to cover the 11,123 miles between Mildenhall, Suffolk and Melbourne. Another Comet, G-ACSR finished fourth after two airliners. (De Havilland)

This standard **Douglas DC-2**, PH-AJU, of KLM, race no. 44, took second place in the truly-challenging October 1934 England-to-Australia air race. The DC-2 may have taken an additional 20 hours 15 minutes over the winning DH 88 Comet's time, but it did the journey in luxury, carrying a crew of four to combat fatigue, three fare-paying passengers and mail. To add hurt to injury, this aircraft was actually being used for route-proving KLM

services to the then Dutch East Indies (now Indonesia), and as such was required to make all the necessary scheduled stop-overs. Powered by two 875hp Wright Cyclones, the KLM DC-2 used on their Far East service, started on 12 June 1935, initially carried five Passengers and cruised at 168mph. Interestingly, KLM's DC-2s reduced the trip time by a third to six days, of which the flying time was 57hours. (KLM)

The **Bellanca 28-90B Flash** seen here was the original 28-70, first flown on 1 September 1934, with its 700hp engine replaced by a 900hp Pratt & Whitney R-1830 Twin Wasp. As the 28-70, the aircraft had been registered in Ireland as EI-AAZ. Named 'Irish Swoop', the machine had been entered for the October 1934 England-to-Australia air race, but was forced to withdraw on technical grounds. Crashed in 1935, the aircraft was rebuilt

in 1936 with the bigger Twin Wasp added. Registered NR190M 'Dorothy', it was sold to the Spanish Republicans in 1937 and led to an order for a further 20, switched to China following US Government intervention. Persistently, the Spaniards ordered another 22, to be routed via Mexico, but all remained there until the Spanish Civil War had ended. (Bellanca)

Below Triumphant twosome, **Benjamin Odell 'Ben' Howard**, on the right and **Gordon Israel** inspect their 1935 Bendix Trophy winning creation, the Howard DGA 6 'Mr Mulligan'. 'Ben' Howard, born a Texan in early 1904, bought a Standard on hire purchase in 1922 and promptly demolished it attempting to teach himself to fly. Despite this unpromising start, Howard held a commercial pilot' licence by 1923 and became a flying instructor. After a colourful period in which he produced his DGA-2, an aircraft built from bits and pieces to carry 'bootleg booze', Howard settled down to airline flying as a living in 1928. However, during the late 1929-early 1930 period, Howard, who had long harboured thoughts of producing his own racer, met up with Gordon Israel, a then 18-year old student of aeronautical engineering, who was to become Howard's collaborator on his series of racers. Israel was to supply much of the detailed design work and also provided constructional supervision, starting with the DGA 3 through to the DGA 6. In 1936 Howard set up his own company to produce a series of 4 and 5 seaters based on the DGA 6, while Gordon Israel went on to join Grumman's Engineering Department.

Very much 'a wolf in sheep's clothing', 'Ben' Howard's sixth 'Damn Good Airplane' was a comfortable four seater touring design of 1934. Perhaps larger than most, it looked like just another in the high-wing lightplane category, that was until it got airborne. Here, it displayed a speed and climb capability greater than that of many contemporary fighters. For example, top level speed was 292mph at 11,000 feet, while sea level cruising was 251mph. Equally impressive for the time was the **DGA 6's** 4,450 feet per minute initial rate of climb. Completed within a four month period, NR273Y, 'Mr Mulligan' had its landing gear and propeller demolished in a forced landing on route to Los

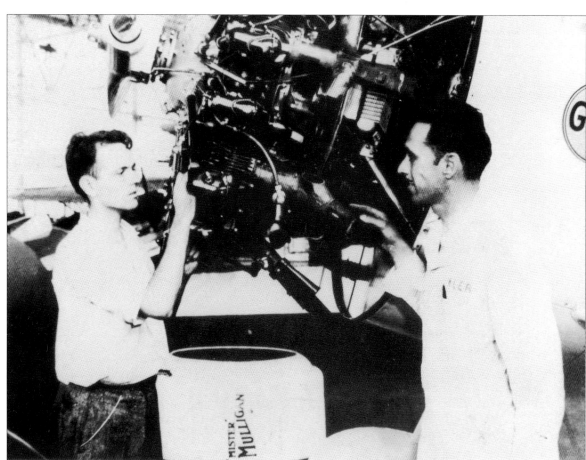

Angeles for the 1934 Bendix start. Repaired in time for the 1935 US Nationals, the DGA 6, race no. 40, romped away with both major prizes. With Gordon Israel along for the ride, 'Ben' Howard flew 'Mr Mulligan' over the 2,043 miles course to take first place in that year's Bendix Trophy, with a speed of 238.704mph. Flown by Harold Neumann in the 1935 Thompson, NR273Y, again came in first, with a speed of 220.194mph. Power for 'Mr Mulligan' was provided by a 830hp Pratt & Whitney Wasp. Incidentally, the prize money for both events totalled $11,250, some $6,500 less than the repair cost of the 1934 damage.

Below Intended to take part in the October 1934 England-to-Australia air race, the all-metal, retractable-wheeled **Keith Rider R-3**, NR14215, started its extended career inauspiciously. Completed too late for timely shipping to England, the R-3 was entered for the 31 August-3 September 1934, US Nationals and the Los Angeles-starting Bendix. Carrying the race no. 9, and flown by James Granger, the R-3 nosed over at the Burbank start for the 2,043 miles opening-day dash to Cleveland, killing its pilot. Rebuilt for the 1935 Bendix and piloted by Earl Ortman in Gilmore Oil livery, the machine got as far as Kansas City before retiring with a damaged engine cowling. Always subsequently flown by Ortman, the R-3 was fitted with various Pratt & Whitney Wasps, varying from 575hp to 900hp. Seen here fitted with a 750hp Wasp Jr. at the start of the 1936 Los Angeles-based National's Thompson event, held on 7 September, Ortman flew the R-3 into second place with a speed of 248.042mph. After winning a string of second place prizes, including the 1937 Bendix and Thompson and the 1938 Thompson, the R-3 ended its racing days after it was placed third in the 1939 Thompson. (US Air Force)

The confident 29-year old **Howard Robard Hughes** stands besides his Hughes H-1, the machine he had conceived, funded and flown to establish a new world landplane speed record of 352.388mph at Santa Ana, California, on 13 September 1935. A natural pilot, socialite, film producer and autocratic multi-millionaire, Howard Hughes had been born towards the end of December 1905. Hughes had the H-1 designed and assembled under the utmost secrecy, ready to enter it for the 1935 Thompson Trophy. When the fraternity of less affluent racing pilots begged him to reconsider he swung his goal towards gaining the world landspeed record, or so this somewhat uncharacteristic story of Hughes goes. Whatever actually happened, Hughes in his H-1 did capture the record and later set a new west-to-east continental crossing record in January 1937. Among his pre-World War II feats was his July 1938

Northern Hemisphere circumnavigation of the globe with his 4-man crew in a Lockheed Model 14 in less than 4 days and his controlling acquisition of TWA. Considered a dilettante by some of the establishment, a maverick by others, Hughes remained steadfastly involved in aviation, including the wartime eight-engined Hughes HK-1 Hercules flying boat and his twin-engined XF-11 fast, long range reconnaissance type. Insisting on making the XF-11's first flight on 7 July 1946, things went awry due to a propeller malfunction that slewed the large machine and its pilot into a Hollywood suburb. Despite the total destruction of the first XF-11 and his own severe injuries, Hughes recovered to make the first flight in a modified second example of the same design on 5 April 1947. While his eccentricities multiplied in the following years, it is difficult to attribute them to his crash, particularly as he continued to sometimes fly his airline's 4-engined Lockheed Constellations single-handedly to-and-fro across the US for some years. The origin of his decline in later years was far more likely to have pre-dated his crash, rather than been caused by it. (Hughes)

The **Seversky SEV-3M**, (N)X15391, was a two seat development of the three seat SEV-3XAR amphibian. Company founder, Major Alexander de Seversky had already piloted the SEV-3XAR to set a new speed record for amphibious aircraft of 179.576mph on 9 October, 1933. A year and eleven months later, on 15 September 1935, de Seversky beat his own record, flying the 710hp Wright R-1820-F3 Cyclone-engined SEV-3M, at a speed of 230.413 mph. (Republic Aviation)

Below First flown on 17 August 1935, the sole **Hughes H-1**, NR258Y, was of fairly conventional construction, but set new standards in its surface smoothness. Equipped with a 700hp take-off rated Pratt & Whitney R-1535-SA1G, this supercharged engine provided 1,000hp at altitude. As initially flown, the H-1 was fitted with a 25 feet span wing and it was with this that Hughes reached his 352.388 mph to set a new world landplane speed record on 13 September 1935. Later, the H-1 had its racing wing removed and replaced by a 31 feet 6 inch wing for long range flying *(above right)*. It was with this wing, that Hughes flew the H-1 from the west to east coast on 17 January, 1937, to set a new US crossing record time of 7 hours 28 minutes 10 seconds. The H-1's chief designer was Richard Palmer, who was to replace Gerald R. Vultee at the company bearing his name when Vultee was killed in an air crash. (Hughes)

Bottom The **De Havilland Technical School TK 2** was a classic example of a design that not only shrank, it simultaneously switched roles from being a tandem, two seat tourer into a single seat racer. First flown on 16 August 1935, with Capt. Hubert Broad at the controls, the sole example. G-ADNO, was entered for the 1935 King's Cup air race to be held at Hatfield, Hertfordshire, on 6-7 September. Allocated race no. 18, Broad flew the TK 2 into fourth place at a speed of 168.88mph. Even then the second seat had been removed to make way for a fuel tank. For the 1936 racing season, G-ADNO was fully converted into a dedicated single-seat racer, with a new cockpit canopy and a lower profile on the upper fuselage. In the King's Cup of 1936, the TK 2 was placed sixth, with a speed of 172.05mph, whilst for the 1938 King's Cup, the machine was further modified with a reduced wingspan, as seen here. Flown throughout the 1938 season by Flg. Off. Geoffrey de Havilland the younger, the TK 2 won the London to Cardiff race, held on 10 September, at a speed of 187.5mph. Over its career, the TK 2 was fitted with DH Gipsy Majors of several marks, with ratings from 142hp to 137hp. (De Havilland)

Above right Roscoe Turner with his **Wedell-Williams**, NR61Y, race no. 57, just prior to the 1935 Bendix. On this occasion Turner was placed second, covering the 2,043 miles at a speed of 238.522mph and landing less than half a minute behind the winning Howard DGA 6 'Mr Mulligan' that had needed only one refuelling stop, compared with three made by the lower altitude-flying Wedell-Williams, by now fitted with a 1,000hp Pratt & Whitney R-1690 Hornet. (Turner)

Designed as a fast feederliner, or executive transport, the **British Aircraft B.A. 4 Double Eagle** had accommodation for a pilot, plus up to five passengers First flown in mid-June 1936, the first of the three examples built used two 130hp DH Gipsy Majors, while the later machines, of which the second,

G-AEIN, is seen here, both wore twin 200hp DH Gipsy Six. G-AEIN is carrying the 1936 King's Cup race no. 4, it came third. with a speed of 151.5mph.

Above Typifying the differing approaches adopted to air racing between the US and Europe is this photograph of a four-engined, 10-passenger **Short Scion Senior**, G-AECU, race no. 19, being flown in the September 1937 King's Cup air race by Short's Harold Piper. Under the European system of aircraft handicapping, aircraft of this size and lack of alacrity still had a chance of competing against the sleek, single-engined, single-seat out-and-out racers. In Europe, the handicappers worked to strike a balance between such factors as total installed power versus aircraft weight and other criteria, whereas the American method was to run the events on raw horsepower, which, if nothing else made American air racing much more of a spectator sport. Piper and G-AECU were unplaced. (Shorts)

Below Built specifically for high altitude engine development, the sole **Bristol Type 138A**, K4879, was first flown on 11 May 1936, by the redoubtable Cyril Uwins. Powered by a 500hp Bristol Pegasus P.E.65, the Type 138A set a new world altitude record by climbing to 53,937 feet on 30 June 1937, with Flt. Lt. M. J. Adams at the controls. A second Type 138, L7037, had its airframe completed as a two-seater, but the proposed installation of a Rolls-Royce Kestrel was never completed. (Bristol)

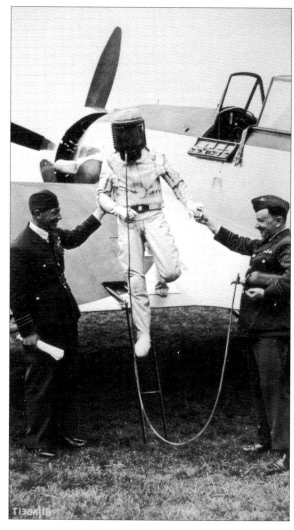

A revealing view of the partially pressure-suited **Flt. Lt. M. J Adams** descending from the cockpit of the Bristol Type 138A. (British Aerospace)

Above From ugly duckling to swan. During March 1934, the London-based, ex-patriate Australian, Capt. Edgar **Percival**, took off on the maiden flight of his new racer, the **Mew Gull**, G-ACND. At this time the machine was far from beautiful and gave the appearance of being tail heavy. Subsequently destroyed during October 1935, the aircraft was rebuilt into a much more pleasing shape. Overall, the new shape was reminiscent of the Caudron C-366 of early 1933, particularly, as seen here, with its initial 180hp Regnier engine used to take part in a French air race. Later, G-ACND was to be fitted with a 200hp DH Gipsy Six that gave the machine a top level speed of 225mph. This aircraft and the other Mew Gulls were to dominate the British air racing scene throughout the latter half of the 1930s. (Percival)

First flown in the spring of 1934, the exceptionally sleek, retractable-wheeled **Caudron C-460** was the ultimate in a line of single-seat Caudron racers designed by Marcel Rifford and his team. Initially, the C-460's proved a disappointment, with two of the three C-460s entered for the 27 May 1934 Coupe Deutsch failing to complete the event, while even the survivor could do no better than third place, behind a C-450 and C-366, both with fixed wheels. Key to the C-460's subsequent success flowed from the constant improvement in power output from the machine's 485.7 cubic inch swept-volume, supercharged Renault R-428. On 25 December 1934, a C-460, flown by Raymond Delmotte, set a new world landspeed record in its engine class of 314.188mph. The following spring, the same pilot took first place in the 1935 Coupe Deutsch, averaging 275.7mph. On 24 August 1935, Delmotte flew a C-460 to set a new 1,000 kilometre, or 621 miles, closed circuit speed record of 279.5mph. Just under a year on and a C-460 was shipped to the US to take part in the 1936 US Nationals, held that year in Los Angeles between 4–7 September. Here, ironically, if the racing fraternity had not pressed Howard Hughes and his Hughes H-1 to stay away, the C-460 might have had some real opposition. As it was the C-460, race no. 100, with its pilot Michel Destroyat, roared home to take first place in both the Greve and the Thompson Trophies at 247.3mph and 261mph, respectively. After that foreign visitors were not welcome at the National. (TRW)

Opposite **Frank Monroe Hawks**, born in Iowa, is seen here standing in front of the fourth of five Travel Air Model Rs to be built, his was the Texaco-owned NR1313, Texaco no. 13. Hawks specialised in point-to-point flying, setting speed records between cities. In May and June 1931 Hawks brought 'Texaco no. 13' to Europe and added a host of record flights between pairs of cities, such as his time of 59 minutes between London and Paris. Retiring from air racing in 1937, Hawks was killed on 23 August 1938, when the Gwenn Aerocar he was demonstrating hit overhead power lines and crashed. (Texaco)

Below The **Hawks Aircraft 'Time Flies'**, R1313, was designed by Howell Miller, who had taken over as the Granville Brothers' Chief Designer after 'Bob' Hall had moved on. Later, Miller maintained something of the old Granville Brothers' organisation and was approached by Frank Hawks to produce 'Time Flies', funded by the Gruen Watch Company. With Hawks providing the machine's demanding specifications, work got underway to complete the aircraft in time for the 1936 US Nationals. With its 1,150hp Pratt & Whitney Twin Wasp giving a top level speed of around 375mph, the 'Time Flies' carried sufficient fuel to fly 1,700 miles and was seen to have the potential to win both the Bendix and the Thompson. All these expectations were to evaporate when Frank Hawks wrecked the retractable landing gear and cracked a main wing spar in a crash landing during pre-race testing. Note the extendible cockpit canopy which, with the pilot's seat, was raised for take-off and landing and lowered to lie flush with the upper fuselage contours in cruising flight. Following the mishap, the aircraft was repaired and was flown in the 1938 Thompson as the Military Aircraft Corporation HM-1 without success. It ended its days in an in-flight aerobatics-induced break-up, from which the pilot, Earl Ortman, bailed out and parachuted to safety. (US Air Force)

Above 'All that glitters is not gold', as the old saying goes and the prototype **Breda Ba 88** offers a prime example of just such an

instance. First flown in October 1936 by Breda's Chief Test Pilot, Furio Niclot, this two-seat fighter-bomber and reconnaissance type was initially flown with a single fin and rudder, in early 1938 it was modified to take the twin-finned tail unit shown here. Powered by two 900hp Gnome-Rhone K14 Mistrel Majors, the sleek prototype certainly impressed the aviation community with its series of closed circuit speed records during 1937. In April of that year, the Ba 88 averaged 321,25mph and 295.15mph over 100 and 1,000 kilometre courses, respectively. In December 1937, the Ba 88 bettered its own times over the same distances, with speeds of 344.24mph and 325.60mph. Clearly flown under ideal conditions, the prototype was always only marginally stable. To cure this problem, the production aircraft used twin-finned tails and wing leading-edge slots, plus an increase in engine power with twin 1,000hp Piaggio P.XI RC.40s, but these remedies only seemed to make matters worse and the production machines were rapidly withdrawn from service in the latter part of 1940. (Breda)

Overleaf The sixth and last **Percival Mew Gull** to be built, G-AFAA, was readied in time to compete in the 1937 King's Cup. Flown in the race by its designer/pilot, Capt. Edgar Percival, the machine was placed third with the race's fastest speed of 238.7mph, while the handicappers placed the slower Mew Gulls of Charles Gardner and Giles Guthriet into first and second places, respectively. This evocative photograph, taken by wartime ferry pilot, C. W. Rodgers, shows G-AFAA at the start of the 1938 King's Cup, in which it wore the race no. 23. Again

flown by Capt. Percival, this time the machine was placed sixth. This last Mew Gull actually differed significantly from the earlier five, having a narrower fuselage, shorter wingspan and the later 205hp DH Gipsy Six II. (C.W. Rodgers)

Right Designed on the old principle of building the minimum airframe to house a normal size pilot, engine and fuel, the **De Havilland Technical School TK 4** was powered by a 137hp DH Gipsy Major Srs 2. Equipped with retractable main wheels and Handley Page automatic wing leading-edge slots, the TK 4's construction used a combination of spruce and balsa with plywood as the main skinning material. First flown on 30 July, 1937, the brightly red painted sole example, G-AETK had an impressive measured top level speed of 244mph at 1,500 feet, along with a full throttle range of 450 miles. Shown here wearing its 1937 King's Cup race no. 1, that year's handicappers placed it ninth with a speed of 230.5mph. Sadly, tragedy was to strike within weeks of the race, when on 1 October, while practising for a speed record attempt, the machine crashed on the edge of Hatfield aerodrome, killing De Havilland Test Pilot, R. J. Waight. (De Havilland)

Below right Built in 1936, the retractable wheeled **Keith Rider R-4**, R261Y, was initially powered by a 250hp Menasco B6S, with which Roger Don Rae flew it into third place in that year's Thompson Trophy wearing race no. 70. Its speed over the gruelling 15-lap, 150-mile Thompson course was 236.559mph, some 11mph faster that the 225.544mph it had notched up to win first place with the same pilot in the previous day's Shell Dash event. For the 1937 season, the machine was re-engined with the

much more potent 400hp Menasco C6S. By now its ownership had changed to C. H. 'Gus' Gotch, who adorned it with its 'Schoenfeldt Firecracker' identity and flew it into third place in the 1937 Greve Trophy, with a speed of 231.593mph. Still retaining its race no. 70 and 'Schoenfeldt' identity, the R-4 was flown into first place in the 1938 Greve event by A. W. 'Tony' Le Vier, with a speed of 250.886mph. Again flown by Le Vier in the 1939 Thompson Trophy, R-4 took a creditable second place, clocking 272.538mph, some 10mph slower than the winning 1,000hp L-RT of third time Thompson winner, Roscoe Turner. As seen here, the R-4 has already been re-engined and is at Burbank, the site of the 1937 US Nationals. (Lockheed)

Bottom Designed initially as an airliner, the vivid performance of **Savoia-Marchetti's SM 79**, first flown in late 1934, soon saw its adoption as a bomber. During 1937 and early 1938, selected crews of the Italian Air Forces' No. 12 Stormo, the 'Sorci Verdi', or Green Mice, flew their SM 79Ts on a series of spectacularly fast, long range flights. These culminated in a three 'plane Rome to Rio de Janeiro trip, involving one refuelling stop at Dakar on the west African coast. Commanded by Col. Attilio Biseo, one of the trio, I-BRUN seen here, was piloted by Bruno Mussolini, son of the Italian dictator. While one of the trio dropped out at Natal, on Brazil's north eastern coast, both Biseo's and Mussolini's aircraft made it to Rio de Janeiro on 25 January 1938, having covered 6,121 miles in 22 hours 40 minutes, representing an average speed of 251mph. (Italian Air Ministry)

Another great photograph from the album of C.W. Rodgers that captures all the tension and vitality of the start of an air race, this time depicting modified **Percival Mew Gull**, G-AEXF, the mount of Alex Henshaw and outright winner of the 1938 King's Cup with a speed of 236.25mph. Henshaw's machine, race no. 22, was followed home that year by another Mew Gull, G-AEKL,

race no. 21, flown by Giles Guthrie into second place, while Capt. Percival's G-AFAA was placed sixth. Flown over a 50.607 mile triangular course, the 1,012 mile race started and ended at Hatfield, Herfordshire and was held on 2 July. The non-Percival modified G-AEXF of Henshaw featured a 230hp DH Gipsy Six R, new wheel spats and a lowered cockpit canopy. (C.W. Rodgers)

Overleaf **Hendy Heck 2C**, G-AEGI, was, perhaps, typical of the second tier touring type entrants for the 1930s King's Cup air races. This example wears the 1938 King's Cup race no. 11 and, flown by J. A. C. Warren, was placed 10th in that year's event. G-AEGI was the second of five of these 3-seat tourers built by the parent Parnall Company and was powered by a 200hp DH Gipsy Six. (De Havilland)

Below The development of the twice Thompson Trophy winning **Laird-Roscoe Turner**, or L-RT, was convoluted to say the least. First conceived as a bigger-winged Gee Bee Model R-styled machine, the basic plans were drawn up by Howard W. Barlow and John D. Ackerman at the beginning of 1937. These were then supplied to Lawrence Brown, designer and builder of the Brown B-2 'Miss Los Angeles', who was to construct the aircraft. Brown, it is reported, introduced some unauthorised modifications that resulted in a heated argument with Roscoe Turner, who then removed the incomplete aircraft, shipping it across country to the Laird plant just outside Chicago, where it arrived in early June 1937. Completed 10 days before that year's Thompson, to be held on 6 September, luck was against Turner on this occasion, the L-RT, R263Y, race no. 29 was placed third, after having to round a marker pylon twice. Undaunted, Roscoe Turner, flying the L-RT with its big, twin-row 1,100hp Pratt & Whitney R-1830 Twin Wasp, went onto greatness by winning both the 1938 and 1939 Thompson Trophies, to add to the one he had already won in 1934. Turner's winning times in the 1938 and 1939 events were 283.419mph and 282.536mph, respectively. Thus, Turner was to become the only three times winner of the coveted Thompson Trophy. The L-RT is shown here in its 1937 racing trim.

American aviatrix Jacqueline Cochran flew this **Seversky AP-4**, NX1384, race no. 13, to win the 1938 2,043-mile Burbank, California, to Cleveland, Ohio, Bendix Trophy. Averaging 249.744mph, NX1384 was powered by a 1,200hp Pratt & Whitney R-1830-19 Twin Wasp and had a fully-retractable landing gear, as opposed to the semi-retracting gear of the standard Seversky P-35A pursuit type from which it derived. Incidentally, on this occasion, 'Jackie' Cochran continued on from Cleveland to Bendix, New Jersey, to set a new woman's coast-to-coast record crossing time of 10 hours 7 minutes 10 seconds, representing an average speed of 242.088mph.

Below and above right Originally built for Capt. Alex Pappana, who planned to use the three-engined **Bellanca 28-92** for a record-setting trans-Atlantic flight between the US and his native Rumania in mid-1938. This scheme fell through and the former Rumanian registered YR-AHA became NX2433, when sold to its new owner, Frank Cordova. Entered for the 1938

Bendix and flown by Cordova, NX2433, race no. 39, was forced out of the race by engine trouble. Better luck attended the big Bellanca in the following year's Bendix when, flown by Arthur Bussy, it was placed second with an average speed of 244.486mph. On this occasion the machine, as seen here, wore the race no. 99. (Bellanca)

Overleaf The RAF Long Range Development Unit was formed at RAF Upper Heyford, Oxfordshire, during January 1938, using six modified **Vickers Wellesley** bombers, whose high aspect ratio, or long, narrow wings made them an ideal choice for the task. Fitted with an 835hp Bristol Pegasus XXII, complete with automatic boost and mixture control, these Wellesleys also had a new 3-axis autopilot and provided a mass of long range operating experience. Three of these machines were used to establish a new world distance record of 7,157.7 miles flying from Ismailia, Egypt, to Darwin, Australia, on 5-7 November 1938. (Vickers)

Below First flown on 22 January 1938, the prototype **Heinkel He 100V1**, seen here, was an attempt to produce a production fighter superior to the Messerschmitt Bf 109. Just how close the Heinkel design team came to reaching their goal can be gauged from the fact that the reduced wingspanned HE 100V8, D-IDGH, fitted with an 1,800hp special Daimler-Benz DB601, set a new absolute world air speed record of 463.92mph on 30 March 1939. The pilot, on the flight was Heinkel's Hans Dieterle. This feat and the He 100 that achieved it compared very favourably with the barely flyable 2,300hp Me 209, which managed to better the Heinkel's record by a marginal 5.3mph a month later. (Heinkel)

Right and opposite Italian Air Force **Lt. Col. M. Pezzi** prepares for his world aeroplane-altitude record-setting flight of 22 October 1938. His aircraft, seen opposite, was a **Caproni Ca 161bis** and its engine a Piaggio radial. Pezzi ascended to a height of 56,046 feet, a record for piston-engined aircraft that stands to this day. (Italian Air Ministry)

Left and below **Prof. Willy Messerschmitt** reaches into the cockpit of the first prototype **Messerschmitt Me 209**, D-INJR, to congratulate company pilot, Fritz Wendel. The occasion was to mark Wendel's establishing a new absolute world air speed record of 469.22mph on 26 April 1939. Unlike the Heinkel He 100, the Messerschmitt Me 209 was designed specifically and solely to set a new absolute world air speed record. The Me 209 design exhibited what was now becoming the traditional Messerschmitt approach of minimalism. This may

well have produced a powerful, lightweight machine, but the barely adequately-sized flying and control surfaces ensured that the aircraft was 'skittish' in its handling, particularly around its pitching axis, keeping its pilot extremely alert. Flown initially on 1 August 1938, the Me 209V1 was the first of three examples to be built. The engine fitted for the record flight was a special 2,300hp Daimler-Benz DB601ARJ. (Daimler Chrysler Aerospace)

Below Drawn up by Clayton **Folkerts**, his **SK-3** 'Jupiter' and **SK-4** were two examples of the same design and, in turn, closely resembled the SK-2 'Toots' other than in their use of a 400hp Menasco C6S4 in place of 'Toots's' 225hp Menasco C4S. SK-3, R14899, was built for Rudy Kling in time for him to fly it in the 1937 US Nationals. Held that year at Cleveland, Ohio, Kling won the Greve Trophy with a speed of 232.3mph, before going on to win that year's even more prestigious Thompson Trophy at 256.91mph, the SK-3 carried the race nos. 301 and 1 respectively. Kling was to lose his life flying the SK-3 at the annual Miami Air Manoeuvres in December 1937. The SK-4, NX288Y, seen here, was built for Roger Don Rae to fly in the September 1938 US Nationals and allotted race no. 15. Withdrawn when Rae encountered wing flutter, the SK-4 was sold to Delbert Bush. Its new owner was killed when the SK-4 crashed during qualifying trials for the 1939 US Nationals.

Consistent champions, Frank Fuller Jr. and his **Seversky SEV S2**, R/NR70Y, dominated the last three years of the pre-World War II Bendix Trophy events. Essentially a de-militarised Seversky P-35A, the Fuller-flown SEV S2 won the 1937 Bendix with a speed of 258,242mph wearing the race no. 23. In the 1938 Bendix, Frank Fuller Jr., a paint-producing magnate, had to be content with second place behind Jacqueline Cochran's more powerful Seversky AP4. Fuller's race no. that year was '77' and his speed, 238.604mph. In the 1939 Bendix Trophy, Fuller retained the race no. 77 and won the event for a second time with a vivid 282.098mph. As Cochran had done the previous year, Fuller continued on to Bendix, New Jersey, to complete an 8 hour 58 minute 8 second crossing of the continent. (Seversky)

Left and below Conceived by D. Napier and Son Ltd. as a world air speed record-setting showcase for their new 2,000hp class Sabre liquid-cooled 24-cylinder engine, design work on the aircraft to carry it, the **Heston Type 5 Racer**, was not initiated until December 1938. Drawn up by consultant designer A. E. Hagg and Heston's George Cornwall, the Type 5 effort was funded by Lord Nuffield. Of the two examples, G-AFOK and G-AFOL, only the first was completed and flown. Perhaps the most superbly-contoured piston-engined machine of all time, the Type 5 used a thin-sectioned symmetrical wing aerofoil and geared flight controls for ease of handling across the aircraft's speed range. Unfortunately, during its 12 June 1940 maiden flight, Heston's Chief Test Pilot, Sdn. Ldr. G. L. G. Richmond, fearing an engine seizure, inadvertantly stalled the aircraft at a height of around 30 feet, and broke the Type 5's back, when he attempted to make a hasty return to the airfield. According to engine company representatives present, Richmond had been warned not to throttle the Sabre back too much as this would create cooling problems. As the radiator was mounted immediately beneath the cockpit any cooling problems would be rapidly transferred upwards as a heating of the cockpit, which, apparently is what happened and caused Richmond's concern. The Type 5's estimated top level speed was quoted as 480mph. (D. Napier & Son Ltd)

Records Overshadow Racing, 1945–1972

With the war had come the jet and rocket-propelled machines that took aircraft speeds into the regions well beyond the means of a handful of dedicated designers and mechanics, which it seemed was all that had been needed to produce the Gee Bees, Mew Gulls and L-RTs of the 1930s. To compound the problem, Winston Churchill's Fulton speech of 1947 indicated that the threat of war had not yet vanished, America and the USSR came into open dispute over their 'economic annexation' of a war-torn Europe. Then, in 1948, came the Berlin Airlift heralding the onset of a new, technology-driven phenomenon, the so-called Cold War, with aviation, soon to become aerospace, at its head. The aircraft provided a ready means by which to exhibit a nation's military technology. What better way, after all, to demonstrate that your fighter or bomber was faster, or carried more load further, than by using your latest, 'state-of-the-art' machine to establish

some new, operationally impressive record. Little wonder, the aspirant racing aircraft designer/builder had to be content to 're-invent the wheel' in the form of the Le Vier Cosmic Wind, or Cassutt Racer. Air racing may well still be alive and kicking in such places as Reno, Nevada, but it is running largely on machinery that is fifty or more years old, albeit of the more exotic flying variety.

The reason why government-furnished, government-backed record breakers dominate this chapter has already been touched upon, but even here, it is interesting to note how the pace of record-setting reduces with time as the machines approach the limits of the available technology. For example, some of the records established around thirty years or more ago by

the Lockheed SR-71 still stand today. Quite a sobering thought in this, the age of the all-prevailing accountant with their all-important 'bottom line'. Can even a little of the 'Gung-ho' spirit of the men touched upon in this book survive the austere financial strictures of the new breed of 'Zero Budgeting', 'Just-in-time Stock Support' men in suits?

First flown on 6 October 1954, the first of two **Fairey FD 2** supersonic research aircraft, WG774, is seen here. Powered by a 12,000lb s.t. reheated Rolls-Royce Avon R.A.5, this aircraft went on the set a new absolute world air speed record in March 1956, the last time Britain was to hold this 'Blue Riband' of records during the first century of manned, powered flight. (Fairey Aviation)

Above and left Stripped of as many protuberances as possible, along with anything internal that was not of vital importance to the aircraft's flight integrity, the one-off **Lockheed P-80R** stands glistening in its high gloss finish on the apron at Van Nuys, California. Starting life as the ninth P-80A, 44-85200, the aircraft was initially modified to take a thinner airfoil-sectioned wing and more powerful engine, becoming the XP-80B in the process and, equally clearly, once the US Army Air Force had decided to attempt an absolute world air speed record, then the XP-80B was the ideal machine to try for it. Stripped down and smoothed over, the XP-80B was fitted with a drag-reducing minuscule cockpit canopy and had its wingtips cropped, transforming it into the P-80R, where the R signified Racing. In the hands of **Col. Albert Boyd**, Chief of the Flight Test Division, Air Material Command, Wright Field, the P-80R was flown to a new record speed of 623.8mph on 19 June 1947. This picture of Col Boyd portrays not only the man who introduced Charles E. 'Chuck' Yeager to test flying, but also a man equipped to conduct his high speed flying with the added safety of a crash helmet, or 'bone dome', something RAF fighter pilots would not be issued with until well into the first half of the 1950s. (Lockheed and US Air Force)

Opposite top Named 'The Turtle' after part of its nose art, Bu Aer 89082, the first production **Lockheed P2V-1 Neptune** was delivered to the US Navy in September 1946, some sixteen months after the prototype XP2V-1's 17 May 1945 first flight. Bu Aer 89082 ensured its place in aviation history between 29 September and 1 October, 1946, when it covered 11,237 miles in its non-stop flight from Perth in western Australia, to Port Columbus, Ohio. For a long-range, maritime patrol type which the Neptune was, such a distance record proclaimed the type's in-built stamina when it came to endurance, or ability to 'stay on station'. (Lockheed)

Below Another military type that periodically must be seen to have a healthy radius of action is the long-range, escort fighter, used to escort bombers through hostile air space. This helps to explain the new class record set by **North American P-82B Twin Mustang**, 44-65168, 'Betty Jo' on 27-28 February, 1947, when US Army Air Force Lt. Col. Robert E. Thacker and Lt. John Ard flew the aircraft non-stop from Hawaii to New York, a distance of 5,051 miles, flown at a speed of 342mph. This machine was the ninth of 20 P-82Bs delivered in early 1946 and was powered by two 1,300hp Packard-built Rolls-Royce V-1650-23/25 Merlins. Armament comprised six .5in. guns, plus up to four 1,000lb bombs. The two-seater's top level speed was 482mph at 25,000 feet. (US Air Force)

Not all records had to be set by front-line combat types, particularly when it paid to show the nation's resolve to stay ahead in the sphere of applied research, or possibly it was a recurrence of the old Army-Navy rivalry in the case of the 650.9mph absolute world speed record set by US Marine Corps Maj. Marion E. Carl on 25 August, 1947, flying one of the three **Douglas D-558-Is Skystreaks**. (Douglas Aircraft)

Left **Anthony W. 'Tony' Le Vier** pictured here with an early production Lockheed P-80 Shooting Star. Born on 14 February 1913, in Duluth, Minnesota, 'Tony' Le Vier had learned to fly by the time he was fifteen. By 1938, Le Vier had progressed to air racing, where he won the Greve Trophy in the Keith Rider R-4. In the following year, 'Tony' came an honourable second in the unlimited Thompson Trophy, before wiping away the R-4's landing gear on touch-down. Le Vier did a variety of flying jobs before joining Lockheed in April 1941, initially as a ferry pilot, but soon moving into experimental flight testing in 1942. Much of Le Vier's 1943 was spent exploring the compressibiltity problems encountered in diving Lockheed P-38 Lightnings. Remembering this period in a letter he wrote to Aviation Week, 2 March 1970, Le Vier recalled that he dived P-38s around 500 times during these tests, reaching a speed of Mach 0.73, or around 525mph. Le Vier's first flight of a prototype aircraft followed on 10 June 1944, when he went aloft in the first of the two Lockheed XP-80As. It was in escaping from one of this pair that 'Tony' injured himself, after a runaway jet turbine stage sawed its way through the fuselage and left his XP-80A tailless. On a later occasion, Le Vier had the misfortune to shoot himself down. This came about when the Lockheed F-104 Starfighter he was carrying out gun firing testsin, ingested one of its own 20mm cartridges that, in turn, stopped the engine, forcing him to make a 'dead stick', or power-off landing. In all, Le Vier logged 20 proto-type first flights in his years with Lockheed, including those of the XF-94, XF-104, U-2 and, of course, his own Cosmic Wind. Retiring as Lockheed California's Director of Flying Operations in 1974, Le Vier remained actively involved in aviation and particularly flight safety aspects right up to within weeks of his death from cancer in early February 1998. (Lockheed Martin)

Bottom During early 1947, in between his test flying duties with Lockheed, A. W. 'Tony' Le Vier found time to lead a small group of fellow racing enthusiasts in the design and construction of the **Le Vier Cosmic Wind**. Readied in time for that year's first Goodyear Trophy, the two Cosmic Wind entrants 'Minnow', race no. 4 and 'Little Toni', race no. 3, were placed third and fourth, with speeds of 158mph and 157mph. This pair was joined by 'Ballerina', race no. 5, in 1948 and 'Miss Cosmic Wind' in 1949. Powered by an 85hp Continental C85-8FJ, these beautifully groomed, diminutive 18 feet 11.75 inch wing span racers could reach a top level speed of 185mph. Seen here is the third of the five built, N22C, 'Ballerina'. Brought to Britain in 1961, the machine was sold to Norman Jones and his Redhill, Surrey-based Tiger Club, where it resided as G-ARUL. (Cowin Collection)

Hardly recognisable in its ultimate, much modified form is the first **Le Vier Cosmic Wind**, N21C, 'Minnow', still carrying its race no. 4. In its former life, N21C was placed third in the 1947 Goodyear Trophy and won the event in 1948. Following this, N21C was stripped down and rebuilt, as seen here, a process that saw its

single-piece wing moved up to the mid-fuselage position. This meant that the cockpit was moved forward. Not content with this, the whole upper fuselage profile was lowered and a new fin and rudder was fitted. The engine remained the same. (Cowin Collection)

Grp. Capt. John Cunningham, wartime night fighter ace and long time Chief Test Pilot for De Havilland, photographed here about to enter the cockpit of the modified De Havilland Vampire I that he was to fly to a new record height in March 1948. Born in 1917, 'JC' as he was almost universally known by colleagues, entered the De Havilland Technical School in the summer of 1935, shortly afterwards joining No. 604 Squadron, RAF, based at Hendon, on the northwest suburbs of London. While studying aeronautics at Hatfield, 'JC' was learning to fly, initially on an Avro 504N before graduating to Westland Wapitis and Hawker Demons. On completing his studies in 1938, 'JC' was offered and accepted a post by Geoffrey de Havilland the elder, becoming a production test pilot for the DH 94 Moth Minor. It was in early 1939, while accompanying Geoffrey de Havilland the younger in a DH 94, for spin tests that the pair were forced to bail out when the aircraft entered a flat, or auto-rotative, spin. 'JC' recalls that once free of its occupants, the recalcitrant lightplane largely recovered to spiral down too close for the parachutists' comfort. On 23 August 1939, 'JC' rejoined his old unit, N0. 604 Squadron, still at Hendon, but now equipped with the fighter version of the twin-engined Bristol Blenheim I. Thus, 'JC' found himself involved in wartime RAF night/all-weather fighter operations from their very inception and by July 1940 was flying AI, Airborne Interception,

radar-equipped Blenheims from RAF MIddle Wallop, Hampshire. Within two months, No. 604 Squadron had re-equipped with AI carrying Bristol Beaufighter Is and 'JC' was to score his first 'kill' on 20 November 1940. By the following September, 'JC', still in his early twenties, was a Wing Commander, commanding the unit he had joined as an eighteen year old in 1935. In May 1942, during a visit to his unit by King George VI, 'JC', through a combination of skill and stealth managed to turn his 12th 'kill', a Heinkel He 111, into a spectacle watched from the ground by a no-doubt-impressed monarch of the realm. Moving on to command DH Mosquito NF-equipped No. 85 Squadron, 'JC' was promoted to Group Captain in January 1944, aged 27, to take command of Night Operations at 11 Group Headquarters. In November 1945, with a credited 20 'kills', all but one of which were made at night, 'JC' rejoined De Havilland. There 'JC' was to resume his flight test duties, becoming Chief Test Pilot in the wake of the younger Geoffrey de Havilland's untimely death flying a DH 108 in September 1946. Typical of 'JC' was his insistence that he got some big aircraft handling time in prior to his flight testing the DH 106 Comet jetliner and, with Sir Geoffrey de Havilland 'pulling some strings' within BOAC, 'JC' got the couple of hundred hours invaluable experience he felt he needed. John Cunningham eventually retired from Hatfield, by now Hawker Siddeley, in 1980, having made the first flights of the DH 106 Comet, the DH 110 and Hawker Siddeley HS 121 Trident. (De Havilland)

Top Wearing its extended wingtips, this the third production **De Havilland Vampire I,** TG278, was modified to conduct the high altitude flight testing of the company's new 5,000lb s.t. DH Ghost, successor to the standard Vampire's 2,700lb s.t. DH Goblin I. This made the machine an ideal mount with which to assail the existing aeroplane altitude record. First flown in its modified state on 8 May 1947, John Cunningham flew the machine to set a new height record of 59,492 feet on 23 March 1948. As can be seen from the preceding image, gone were the days of needing to wear the cumbersome partial pressure suits of the 1930s, however, the pressurised cockpits of the late 1940s-early 1950s brought their own problems in the shape of the canopy misting up on the inside and even cracking. (De Havilland)

Opposite top **John Derry's** first taste of aviation came at the age of seven, when he went aloft in a Klemm KI 26 at Croydon. Born in December 1921, Derry enlisted into the RAF in September 1939, training as a wireless operator/gunner and served with RAF Coastal Command as such until selected for pilot training in

1943. Even after gaining his wings, it seemed that the young Derry was going to miss taking any active part in the war, as his first duties involved ferry flying with the Air Transport Auxiliary. Happily for him, in October 1944, Derry was posted to an operational Hawker Typhoon squadron and ended his war as a Squadron Leader, commanding No. 182 Squadron, RAF, operating Typhoons in Germany. Prior to leaving the RAF at the end of 1946, Derry had commanded the Hawker Tempest element of the Day Fighter Leaders School at RAF West Raynham, Norfolk. John Derry was invited to join Jeffrey Quill's select group of test pilots with Vicker's Supermarine. Here, Derry found himself responsible for exploring the Supermarine Seafang's high speed handling. It was the skill and analytical judgement he brought to this task that brought John Derry's name to the fore amongst the knowledgeable. Bereft of a timely contract for the Attacker, Jeffrey Quill was approached by De Havilland's John Cunningham, who wished to offer a test pilot' position to Derry. Quill was agreeable and Derry switched to De Havilland in October 1947. His new duties involved exploring the high speed handling of the tailless DH 106. Six months after joining his new firm, in April 1948, Derry set a new 100 kilometre closed circuit speed record of over 605mph in the tricky-to-fly DH 108. Later, in that September, John Derry became the first British pilot to exceed Mach 1 in a British aircraft, when in a nearly catastrophic runaway bunt, his DH 108 tucked it nose down to reach Mach 1.04. John Derry, along with his flight test observer, Tony Richardson, was to be killed on 6 September, 1952, when their DH 110 broke up over the SBAC Show, Farnborough. (De Havilland)

Above The third and last **De Havilland DH 108** Swallow, VW120, powered by a 3,750lb s.t. DH Goblin 4. VW120 was first flown on 27 July 1947 and it was in this aircraft that John Derry, on 12 Apri, 1948, was to set a new 100 kilometre, or 62.2 mile, closed circuit speed record of 605.23mph. VW120 crashed, killing its pilot, Sdn. Ldr. J. S. R Muller-Rowland, head of the RAE's Aerodynamic Flight on 15 February 1950. (De Havilland)

Below Designed by Dave Long, the then Chief Engineer of Piper. the **Long Midget** Mustang, as it was originally known until North American insisted the 'Mustang' be dropped, was aimed at the sportsplane market, to be sold either complete or in kit form. Long built three including NX511H, race no. 67, seen here, that he flew into fourth place in the year end 1949 Miami Air Maneuvres. Sadly, Dave Long was to lose his life shortly afterwards when baling out from the prototype Midget at too low an altitude. Powered by an 85hp Continental C85-8FJ, both the Midget's handling and simplified construction were generally considered superb.

Perhaps because so many **Supermarine** Spitfires were to be retained in service long after the end of World War II, few of the type found their way into air racing. There are always exceptions, however, and this is one of them, a superbly groomed **Spitfire FR XIV**, CF-GMZ, formerly TZ138. Entered for what was to be the last of the Thompson Trophy races in 1949, the machine, race no. 80, flown by James N. G. McArthur, was compelled to drop out during the qualifying heats, but not before averaging 370.110mph. Powered by a 2.050hp Rolls-Royce Griffon 65, the standard Spitfire FR XIV's top level speed was 439mph low down, where this variant of the fighter was meant to operate. (via M. J. Hooks)

Not all records that are set are driven by idealism. One such case was that of the **Supermarine Seagull**. First flown on 14 July 1949, the Seagull was an attempt to prolong the Supermarine line of amphibious aircraft that extended back through the Walrus to their Sea Eagle of 1923. Unfortunately for Supermarine, the Seagull, with its fuel hungry 1,815hp

Rolls-Royce Griffon 29, may have had some innovative ideas, like a variable-incidence wing, but its protracted development saw its arrival coincide with the broadening acceptance of the helicopter as the primary tool for search and rescue duties, the role for which the Seagull had been designed. Thus, despite Supermarine's Leslie Colquhoun flying PA147 to set a new amphibious aircraft 100 kilometre, or 62.2 mile, closed circuit speed record of 241.9mph on 22 July 1950, not a solitary sale followed. Seen here is PA147's sole sister, the prototype Seagull, PA143. (V.A. Supermarine)

Squadron Leader Neville Duke, seen here in the cockpit of an early Hawker Hunter, the aircraft for whose flight testing he was responsible and which brought him to the public's attention. Duke had joined the Hawker company in August 1948, after spending an interesting eight years in the RAF, including flying with No. 112 Squadron in North Africa before going on to command No. 145 Squadron flying North American Mustangs in Italy. Prior to this Duke had flown various marks of Curtiss P-40s since leaving the UK in November 1941. Duke's

wartime flying amounted to 712 hours, 486 operational sorties, 28 'kills' and 3 'probables' In June 1945, Duke was to have his first contact with Hawker, when he was attached to them for test flying duties for a year. This tour of duty completed, Duke took the exacting Empire Test Pilot School course, prior to joining his old squadron companion, 'Wimpy' Wade, then Chief Test Pilot of Hawker, in August 1948. Duke became Chief Test Pilot himself on the death of Wade in April 1951. Just over three months later, on 20 July, Duke took the glistening prototype Hawker Hunter aloft for its first flight. A little over two and a half years later, he was to take the same, albeit modified Hunter aloft to set new records for absolute speed and speed over a 100 kilometre, or 62.2 mile, closed circuit. In August 1951 Neville Duke was to injure his spine in crash landing a Hunter and this was to become progressively more debilitating with time. In August 1956, Duke handed the company Chief Test Pilot reins over the 'Bill' Bedford. Despite this setback, Neville Duke continued his active involvement in flight test work for many more years, if, necessarily on less demanding aircraft, such as the Dowty ducted fanned Britain Norman Islander and the Edgley Optica. (Hawker)

WB188, the prototype **Hawker Hunter** that Sdn. Ldr. Neville Duke had flown on its maiden flight of 20 July 1951, seen here modified to take a 9,600lb s.t. reheated Rolls-Royce Avon R.A.7R. On 7 September 1953, Neville Duke flew this machine, the sole Mk. 3, to set a new absolute world air speed record of 727.642mph. Twelve days later, on 19 September, Duke used the same aircraft to establish a new world 100 kilometre, or 62.2 mile, closed circuit record speed of 709.232mph. (Hawker)

Neville Duke's world air speed record in the Hawker Hunter was to last less than three weeks as a result of the bitter rivalry that then existed between Hawker and Vicker's Supermarine Division. The stakes were high and Duke's Hunter record was stacking the cards in Hawker's favour. To redress the situation, the Supermarine team, led by their Chief Test Pilot, Lt. Cdr. M. J. 'Mike' Lithgow, set off for Libya in order to benefit from the higher temperature, where, on 25 September 1953, Lithgow, flying a **Supermarine Swift F.4** using the same reheated Rolls-Royce Avon as the Hunter, reached 727.702mph. This new absolute world air speed record beat Duke's by a whisker over the mandatory 1 per cent required and was only to last a matter of days. (Vickers)

First flown in 1954, the **Cassutt Racer** was designed by airline captain, Thomas K. Cassutt to the US Formula 1 guidelines which stipulated various not-to-exceed criteria. Capable of being produced complete or in kit form, the Cassutt, which won the 1958 Formula 1 Championship, could be powered by a range of engines from 85hp to 115hp. Top level speed was cited as 230mph. The example shown here, G-AXEA, race no. 40, was the second of three Cassutts built by Airmark Ltd. of London in 1969 and wore a 90hp Rolls-Royce built Continental. (Airmark)

The second Prototype **Douglas XF4D–1 Skyray**, Bu Aer 124587, was the first ever carrier-going aircraft to set an absolute world air speed record. This it achieved on 3 October 1953, reaching 752.944mph in the hands of US Marine Corps Lt. Col. James B. Verdin, A little later in the month, on the 16th, Douglas's own Project Test Pilot, Robert O. Rahn, set a new world 100 kilometre, or 62.2 mile, closed circuit speed of 728.110mph. Both of these records were set when the prototype Skyrays were powered by the unreliable 11,600lb s.t. reheated Westinghouse YJ40-WE-8, production Skyrays used the 13,500lb s.t. Pratt & Whitney J57-P-2. (Douglas Aircraft)

Right Acknowledged as being the world's first fighter capable of level supersonic flight, North American's YF-100A had demonstrated this capability during its 25 May 1953, first flight. Thus, it was no surprise, when on 20 August 1955, A **North American F-100C**, similar to the one seen here, set the world's first supersonic speed record at 822.135mph. The pilot on this occasion was US Air Force Col. Horace A. Hanes. This event was also notable for being the first to be flown at high altitude, where the jet works best. Power for the F-100C was provided by a 16,000lb s.t. reheated Pratt & Whitney J57-P-21. (North American)

The aeroplane altitude record-breaking modified **English Electric Canberra B 2**, WK163, equipped with a 4,000lb thrust Napier Double Scorpion rocket booster engine in its bomb bay. Built as one of a 75 aircraft batch by Avro, WK163 was converted by D. Napier and Son at Luton during 1955. On 28 August 1957, WK163, flown by Napier's Michael Randup and flight test observer W. Shirley, set their new record of 70,308 feet just south of the Isle of Wight. Significantly, the Double Scorpion's thrust, which coming from a rocket remained constant, overtook the combined thrust of the machine's twin Rolls-Royce Avons that fell off in the thinning air at around 50,000 feet. (D. Napier & Son Ltd)

Top right **Lt. Cdr. Peter Twiss**, Chief Test Pilot of Fairey Aviation photographed here at the time of his setting a new absolute world air speed record with the Fairey FD 2 in March 1956. Twiss had joined the Royal Navy, learning to fly in 1940. As a Sub-Lt., he had been posted to fly catapult-launched Sea Hurricanes from the forward decks of hastily converted merchantmen. Produced to counter the threat of the long ranged Focke-Wulf FW 200s being used to stalk British convoys far out into the Atlantic, flying duties aboard these so-called CAM ships called for bravery of a high order, as the Sea Hurricane pilot had nowhere to go other than into a hostile Atlantic if his machine was launched beyond the range of the nearest land base. Twiss was extremely lucky in that on both occasions he was launched he was within range of Belfast or Gibraltar. After this, his 1942 spent flying Fulmars and Supermarine Seafires from British carrier decks in the Mediterranean must have seemed relatively relaxing. In 1944, less onerous duties took the shape of a posting to Washington DC with the British Purchasing commission, followed by attending the Empire Test Pilots School at Boscombe Down. Peter Twiss was first attached to Fairey Aviation in 1946, to assist with problems being experienced with the Firefly. This led to him resigning his commission to join Gordon Slade as his deputy. Twiss, who had already made the first flight of the Fairey FD 2, on 6 October 1954, become the company's Chief Test Pilot on Gordon Slade's retirement from flight testing at the beginning of 1956. On 10 March 1956, Peter Twiss, in the Fairey FD 2 became the last British pilot of the 20th Century to set a new absolute world air speed record. After Fairey Aviation's government enforced absorption by Westland, Peter Twiss switched elements, quitting test flying in 1960 to become Manager of Fairey Marine. (Fairey Aviation)

First flown on 6 October 1954, **Fairey FD2**, WG774 was the first of two examples built. Designed to explore aircraft handling in the supersonic speed region, the FD 2 was powered by a 12,000lb s.t. reheated Rolls-Royce Avon RA 5. Responsible almost single-handedly for the FD 2's flight test and development, Peter Twiss set a new absolute world air speed record in this machine on 10 March 1956, reaching 1,132.136mph. This beat the previous record of 822.135mph, held by the North American F-100C Super Sabre by nearly 38 per cent. (Fairey Aviation)

Initially delivered to the US Air Force Tactical Air Command's 27 Tactical Fighter Wing in the spring of 1957, the big **McDonnell F-101A Voodoo**, with its twin 15,000lb s.t. reheated Pratt & Whitney J57-P-13s carried four 20mm cannons to defend itself while, if necessary, delivering either of the two tactical nuclear weapons then available. The F-101A's dash speed capability was graphically demonstrated by US Air

Force Maj. Adrian E. Drew on 12 December 1957, when he set up a new absolute world air speed record of 1,207.633mph. Seen here is F-101A, 53-2423, a near sister of 53-2426 flown by Drew. (McDonnell)

All sound and fury as one of the two **Sud Ouest SOb9050 Trident IIs** thrusts ever faster under the impulse of its twin barrelled SEPR rocket motor. This aircraft carries a mock-up of a long range air-to-air missile. On 2 May 1958, this mixed rocket- and jet-powered, rapid response interceptor prototype set a new world aircraft altitude record for non-air-launched machines of 79,452 feet. (GIFAS)

Above **Lockheed's F-104 Starfighter** may well be known as the world's first operational Mach 2 fighter, but not in its initial F-104A form, which was limited to Mach 1.57, or 1,037mph at 36,000 feet and above. This appears wrong when it is realised that one of the 17 YF-104As set a new absolute world air speed record of Mach 2.125, or 1,404mph, on 15 May 1958. The explanation is that while the standard F-104A carried a single 14,800lb s.t. reheated General Electric J79-GE-3B, the development aircraft identified by the 'Y' prefix were used to test the latest, increased thrust engines fresh off the manufacturer's test bed. (US Air Force)

Overleaf The **Nord Griffon II** seen here in its landing configuration, was photographed from an accompanying Isrty-based Gloster Meteor chase 'plane. On 25 February 1959, this somewhat ponderous looking dual-cycle jet-cum-ramjet machine, with Andre Turcat at the controls set a new 100 kilometre, or 62.2 mile, closed circuit world air speed record of 1,018mph. In fact, Turcat at this time was flying the Griffon II to speeds of Mach 2.3, or 1,519.442mph, for brief periods at 36,000 feet, the limiting factor not being available power, but the thermal effects on critical parts of the airframe. (GIFAS)

Right The **Sukhoi SU-9 Interceptor**, first flown in 1955, was a contemporary of the Mikoyan Mig-21. This was the period when high flying US spy 'planes were penetrating Soviet air space relatively routinely. It should therefore come of no great surprise to find the Russians laying on some form of counter-capability and this came on 14 July 1959, when a Sukhoi Su-9 zoom-climbed to a new world altitude record of 94,659 feet. Less than a year later, on 28 May 1960, another Su-9 broke the previous 100 kilometre, or 62.2 mile, closed circuit speed record, reaching 1,299.906mph under the thrust of its 22,046lb s.t. reheated AL-7 turbojet.

Son of **Convair's** F-102, the single 24,500lb s.t. reheated Pratt & Whitney J57-P-17 powered **F-106A** was first flown on 26 December 1956. A dedicated all-missile equipped, all-weather interceptor, the F-106A set a new absolute world air speed record of 1,525.95mph, or Mach 2.31, at 36,000 feet on 15 December, 1959. At the controls for this flight was US Air Force Maj. Joseph W. Rogers. Seen here is 56-452, the second of 277 F-106As built, along with 63 of the two-seat F-106Bs. (Convair)

Overleaf **McDonnell's** two-seat **F4H-1**, later F-4A Phantom II, with its twin 17,000lb s.t. reheated General Electric J79-GE-8 turbojets established a string of records between December 1959 and April 1962. Some of the more spectacular feats included a zoom climb to 98,557 feet on 6 December 1959, along with an absolute world air speed record of 1,606.342mph on 22 November 1961. It is of particular interest to compare the F4H-1's 24 May 1961, trans-continental crossing time of 2 hours

49 minutes 9.9 seconds with some of the crossing times of the 1930s. Incidentally, the latter time won the Bendix Trophy for the US Navy VF-121 crew that made the Los Angeles to New York dash (McDonnell)

Below America's first supersonic strategic bomber, **Convair's B-58A Hustler,** set new records for speed and altitude with warload, but proved tricky to fly and downright lethal when its complex, but vital, flight control system failed, as it sometimes did. Typical of the B-58A's feats was its 3,669 mile dash from New York to Paris in 3 hours 19 minutes 41 seconds on 10 May 1961. This flight won its three-man US Air Force crew the Aero Club de France's Louis Blériot Trophy. Tragically, both the aircraft and its crew were to be lost when it crashed on its return flight to the US. Flying B-58s could be hazardous to your health as the statistics show, 26 of the total 116 built were lost by the time the bomber was withdrawn from service at the start of 1970. (Convair)

Opposite top The massive **Mil Mi-6**, first flown in early 1957, was the biggest and heaviest helicopter of its day and while the example seen here, photographed by the author at the Turin Air Show in June 1968, carries Aeroflot markings, most Mi-6s were flown by the Soviet military. Used to spearhead, and later support, heavy assault operations the Mi-6 was powered by two 5,500shp Soloviev D-25V turboshaft engines, giving the helicopter a dash speed of 186mph and a cruising speed of 155mph. In terms of load hauling capability, the Mi-6 could lift a 13,330lb cargo over a distance of 404 miles. The Mi-6 started setting helicopter load lifting records in October 1957, but really impressed the world with its 1,000 kilometre, or 622 mile, closed circuit speed record for helicopters of 186.64mph, set on 15 September 1962, having two days previously lifted a 44,350lb load to an altitude of 8,983 feet. On both occasions, the machine was flown by Mil's R. I. Kapreljan. (Hugh W. Cowin)

Below Although not publicly revealed until early 1964, the first of **Lockheed's** brutally powerful **YF-12A interceptors** had first flown almost two years previously on 28 April 1962. Embodying much of the accumulated technology developed for the high performance X 'planes programmes, the YF-12A was provided with a sustained supersonic cruise capability thanks to its two huge 32,500 s.t. dual cycle jet/ramjet Pratt & Whitney J58 turbo-fans. On 1 May 1965, US Air Force Col. Robert L. Stephens and Lt. Col. Daniel Andre set a number of records, including a new world absolute air speed record of 2,070.099mph, along with a record for sustained level flight at an altitude of 80,257.863 feet. Although the US Air Force deemed the YF-12A too expensive, at a reported $33 million each, to develop as a front-line inter-ceptor, its basic engine/airframe combination was to be utilised in the shape of the SR-71 Mach 3 spy 'plane. (Lockheed)

At the time of its first appearance in 1968 the mammoth **Mil Mi-12** was, and still is, by far the largest helicopter ever built. Powered by four 6,500shp Soloviev D-25VF turboshaft engines, this 3-crew twin-rotored giant set a number of load lifting records during 1969. On 22 February 1969, Mil's V. P. Koloshenko took the Mi-12 to a height of 9,682 feet with a payload of 66,139lb, setting new payload lifting records of 44,092lb and 55,116lb in the process. On 6 August 1969, the same pilot climbed the Mi-12 to 7,382 feet carrying a payload of 88,636lb.

Above The late 1960s and early 1970s appear to have been Russia's time for record-setting and not all were confined to high-performance combat types or helicopters, as shown by this workhorse of Soviet anti-submarine warfare, the 6-crewed **Beriev Be-12** amphibious flying boat. The last of its species to remain operational, the Be-12 was powered by two 4,000eshp PTL AL-20D turboprops, the aircraft setting a number of record for both seaplanes and amphibians during the four years from 1968 to 1972. On 25 April 1968, the Be-12 showed something of its ability to transit from base to wherever needed when it set a new class 500 kilometre, or 310.7 mile, closed circuit record speed of 351.29mph. Perhaps even more impressive was the Be-12's 345.972mph 2,000 kilometre, or 1,242.7 mile, class closed circuit speed record, set on 31 October, 1972.

Below right This much modified **Hawker Sea Fury FB 11**, N878M, 'Miss Merced' stands with its 2,480hp Bristol Centaurus 18 ready to 'burn and turn' in this 1970 photograph of the machine. The third of a 37 aircraft production batch, this aircraft had started life as Hawker Sea Fury FB 11, WG567, one of those supplied to the Royal Canadian Navy, with which it operated until February 1957. The machine then appears on the Canadian Register as CF-VAN between September 1961 and 1965, from whence it crossed the border into the US to become N878M, owned by Michael D. Carrol. In 1969 it passed into the hands of Sherman Cooper, becoming 'Miss Merced', after the Californian town of the same name. By now, as with a host of other surplus piston-engined fighters-cum-racers, the machine had undergone such drastic surgery as to be hardly

recognisable. Notable in the view shown here are the harshly cropped outer wings and the minuscule cockpit canopy. Despite a forced landing in November 1971, N878M soldiered on, it was rebuilt at Chino, California, between 1980 and 1988 to become 'Super Chief' and was certainly still flying in 1995. (via M. J. Hooks)

Above right In the late 1960s true to its heritage of sponsoring air-minded events, the London-based Daily Mail marked the 50th Anniversary of Alcock and Brown's trans-Atlantic flight by putting up a prize purse for the fastest person to cross the Atlantic in either direction, with the top of the recently completed London Post Office Tower and the top of the Empire State Building in Manhatten as the start/finish points. Clearly, aircraft would have to provide the prime means of transport, supported by a sundry collection of short distance aids of which the motor cycle was prominent. The prize for the overall best trip time, over the easier west-to-east section, went to a Royal Navy McDonnell Phantom II pilot, Lt. Cdr. Brian Davis, with a time of 5 hours 11 minutes 22 seconds on 11 May 1969. However, much of the Royal Navy's thunder had been cheekily stolen nearly a week earlier, when on 5 May, the RAF's Sdn. Ldr. Tom Lecky-Thompson, flying a **Hawker Harrier GR 1** and refuelled on route by Handley Page Victor tankers, flew the more arduous east-to-west leg in 6 hours 11 minutes. Seen here is Lecky-Thompson's Harrier, VX741, departing from its temporary pad in a disused coal yard close to St Pancras station. (British Aerospace)

Index